Historic Parks
& Gardens in Ceredigion

Caroline Palmer
with Penny David & Ros Laidlaw
Introduction by Donald Moore

Contents

Acknowledgements

Compiling a book like this is a collaborative effort and the team owes thanks to many individuals and institutions. It has been particularly useful having the National Library of Wales and the libraries and archives of the University of Wales, Lampeter, Ceredigion County Archive Office and the Carmarthenshire Record Office on our doorsteps. We are especially grateful for the use of pictures marked NLW which are reproduced by permission of Llyfrgell Genedlaethol Cymru/The National Library of Wales.

The members of the Ceredigion Branch Committee have given much support, and particular gratitude is expressed to Michael Norman for his assiduous work in locating sponsors to support this project. Financial assistance, by grant or loan, has been generously given by Ceredigion County Council, Adfywio, Cadw: Welsh Historic Monuments, the Ethel and Gwynne Morgan Trust and the Committee of the Welsh Historic Gardens Trust. Branch funds have also been contributed.

Owners and residents of the Ceredigion properties, scholars and other professionals have been helpful in many ways. We record our thanks, among others, to Cecilia Barton, Tony Brothers, Stephen Briggs, Arthur Chater, Penny Condry, Helen Davies, Howard Davies, Peter Davis, Philip Ellis, Denys Evans, Dorothy Evans, Mair Lloyd Evans, Nicky Evans, Edward Fitzwilliam, Michael Freeman, Loveday Lewes Gee, Robert Gee, Sir Timothy Harford, Sylvia Heidrich, Linda Hood, Peter Jenkins, Shirley Jenkins, Glen Johnson, Lord Lisburne, Tom Lloyd, Lionel Madden, Mary Madden, Jennie Macve, Keith Mitchell, Phyllida Mould, Joy Neal, Julian Orbach, Morfydd Owen, Helen Palmer, Tim Palmer, Ian Parrott, Arvid Parry Jones, Bettina Piper, Robert Reen, Joan Reen, Ulrich Roth, Malcolm Slater, Lolly Stalbow, Catherine Usher, Donald Usher and Mrs Stephen Watkins.

We are also grateful to the printers, Y Lolfa, and especially to designer Ceri Jones for his unfailing patience and skill.

First published in 2004 by the Ceredigion Branch of the Welsh Historic Gardens Trust
c/o Coed Glantawe, Esgairdawe, Llandeilo SA19 7RT tel/fax 01558 650735

ISBN 0-9547525-0-3

Designed by Ceri Jones. Printed by Y Lolfa, Talybont, Ceredigion SY24 5AP

Introduction:
Ceredigion and its Gardens

This book is a celebration of the garden history of Ceredigion – the former Cardiganshire. It is also the celebration of a process of discovery. Less than twenty years ago, in 1986, *The Oxford Companion to Gardens* stated that there were hardly any historic gardens of note in Wales. Elisabeth Whittle's *Historic Gardens of Wales* rectified that in 1992, but even she mentioned only four Ceredigion sites: Derry Ormond, Hafod, Nanteos and Trawsgoed. An immense heritage of gardens and designed landscapes existed, awaiting revelation.

Enthusiasts among county members of the Welsh Historic Gardens Trust have been exploring the archives and the Ceredigion landscape, and organizing branch excursions to gardens of interest for the last twelve years. By studying maps and literary records – all in the public domain – Ros Laidlaw, branch conservation officer, estimates

The Nash lodge at Nanteos no longer survives.

that there are almost 200 places where gardens must once have existed. A few of these gardens still exist in glory, albeit modified by changing fashions and constraints of cost. Many, however, can only be recognized on the ground by humps and bumps, ruined walls – and perhaps the odd exotic tree – which have survived the ravages of time and neglect. Others exist only in written descriptions, folklore and memory.

The Historic Legacy

Most of the gardens described in this book were once part of the inherited landed estates belonging to gentry families (in Welsh, *uchelwyr*), who lived in mansions on their own land. Some estates are centuries old, though they often changed ownership through marriage or sale and by today have usually shrunk from their original extent.

Every country house would have had productive gardens to sustain its large household with produce for the table; other areas would be designed for pleasure and display. Once we know where these houses stand, or stood, we can begin the search for gardens and garden features related to them. These mansions and their estates have suffered many changes of fortune. Some houses are in ruins; some have been demolished; some have dwindled to no more than farmhouses. Some have been used by institutions and some have been converted into apartments, residential homes or hotels. The gardens and pleasure grounds surrounding them have met equally diverse fortunes.

Besides the houses of old gentry families, some houses and gardens are more 'recent' creations by 19th-century incomers, often professional people, upwardly mobile tradesmen or entrepreneurs from outside the area, some drawn in as investors in the mining industry. The economic and social forces that brought about the creation of these domains are as diverse as those that caused the decline of the old estates. Industrial success, the profits of war, or gambling, are among the reasons that prompted people to buy a parcel of land and build on it a house and garden that displayed the latest in taste and fashion.

3

These gardens, too, have often declined and disappeared under 20th-century buildings. Like the older estates, many of them had walled kitchen gardens and productive greenhouses as well as ornamental plantings, and the traces of these developments can sometimes be found in old photographs, bills and receipts, or indeed on site.

The large estates generated huge quantities of family papers, legal documents, maps, pictures, land transactions and even receipts for plants bought. On the break-up of estates some collections of archives found their way into public repositories such as the National Library of Wales and the Ceredigion Record Office in Aberystwyth. For others the surviving record is haphazard, and the best sources may be confined to sales particulars and old newspapers. Comparing the different Ordnance Survey maps in their larger scales is of immense value for showing changes in gardens in the 19th and 20th centuries, and the tithe maps and their schedules can be helpful, but since these were compiled parish by parish for the calculation of a tax rather than as a complete representation of what existed on the ground, they are of uneven quality for landscape details. The private estate maps that survive, each drawn up on the instruction of a proprietor, showed the extent of a family's possessions and served as an instrument of management. In Ceredigion extant examples date mainly from the later 18th or early 19th centuries.

However, there are pitfalls in trusting pictures, and maps can be misleading. Photographs tell a kind of truth, but paintings are subject to artistic license and the desire to flatter, and garden plans often show proposed features that were never actually created *in situ*. Caroline Palmer's excellent article in *Gerddi* (Vol. II no. 1 1998–9) gives a vivid picture of the perils that beset the researcher who investigates garden history. If her experience is alarming in suggesting that it is impossible to believe any piece of evidence unless it is corroborated by other verifiable facts, there are compensations in the thrill of the chase and the satisfaction of good detective work well done.

The Land of Ceredigion

Ceredigion has existed as a well defined political and administrative unit since it emerged just after Roman times as the *gwlad* of Ceredig, son of Cunedda, a native ruler from north Britain. It became a Norman Marcher lordship, a royal shire, and then the county of Cardigan; for some years in the 20th century it was a district in the county of Dyfed, but it is now an autonomous county again under its ancient name.

Ceredigion's boundaries have remained much the same through the centuries. It is shaped rather like a banana, with its concave side facing the Irish Sea on the west. Geologists describe its landscape as a series of dissected plateaux descending westwards from the Cambrian Mountains in stepped landforms with level horizons. The land is formed of ancient and resistant rocks that have given rise to poor, acidic soils which, with the addition of drift materials, lie in uneven thicknesses. There are also deposits of waterlogged peat. The rivers carry a considerable rainfall to the sea in deeply incised valleys. Some descend steeply to the coastline, although the larger ones open into broad, fertile

A garden flourished beside Strata Florida ruins in the late 19th century. Engraving reproduced from Nicholas (1872).

4

plains as they approach the sea. Two rivers help to define its boundaries – the winding Teifi in the south and the estuary of the Dyfi in the north. In these, and in the mature valleys of the Ystwyth, Rheidol and Aeron, are found most of the old gentry estates and their gardens and pleasure grounds, as the map facing page 1 clearly shows.

Houses and Gardens

There appears to be a dearth of pre 18th-century houses in the county, but early structures often lie hidden within later rebuilding. There would have been gardens in medieval times at the Cistercian monastery of Strata Florida, and the nunnery of Llanllŷr, and even within the walls of castles. Deer parks would also be expected. Early houses with gardens must have existed, and we get an excellent idea of a compact 17th-century garden from the contemporary drawing by Thomas Dineley showing Trawsgoed (see page 81) laid out in formal geometric shapes according to the fashion of the time. The 18th century saw a move away from the formal garden to the 'natural' landscape garden, which meant sweeping away many elaborate parterres, terraces, avenues and canals, leaving scarcely a trace. Hafod is the supreme example of a 'designed landscape' where a natural amphitheatre with a mansion at its centre was skilfully planted and then furnished with pathways, bridges and other picturesque features.

In the late 18th and early 19th centuries many older houses were rebuilt or transformed into fashionable Georgian residences, where the landscape setting was as important as the architecture. Also at this time came the first tourists who recorded their impressions of the Welsh countryside in books of their travels. The writings of Lewis, Malkin, Meyrick, Nicholas and others are the source for the greater part of the names in the list that begins on page 91 of this book, and the references are given in full in the Bibliography on page 94.

Victorian and Edwardian garden fashion, with a return to formality, had an impact on many existing gardens and inspired the pleasure grounds surrounding new villas. Its influence is still visible in the colourful plantings of orderly municipal flower beds in parks in Aberaeron, Aberystwyth, Cardigan and Lampeter.

VICTORIA GARDENS, CARDIGAN.

W.1019

Private Collection

5

Putting Gardens on Record

The current interest in historic gardens owes much to the Welsh Historic Gardens Trust, founded in 1989 (details can be found on the inside back cover). Its work is done to a great extent by individuals in county branches, and the present publication is essentially the result of the initiative and endeavour of members of the Ceredigion branch.

Another development of the last decade is the involvement of government in recording and protecting historic parks and gardens. Cadw/ICOMOS has published successive volumes of the *Register of Historic Parks and Gardens in Wales*, and in July 2002 the sixth and final volume was issued for Carmarthenshire, Ceredigion and Pembrokeshire. This fine publication (see Bibliography) gives plans and systematic descriptions of outstanding examples from those three counties. Eleven sites in Ceredigion have been awarded this level of national status.

Obviously the *Register* gives a certain status not only to the places listed, but also by implication to historic gardens in general. At present it has no legal force, but the hope has been expressed that planning authorities will consult it when forming their policy. Similarly, we hope that the present publication will assist local government officials in the protection of Ceredigion's heritage.

The major part of this volume consists of detailed descriptions of over 30 gardens arranged in alphabetical sequence. Some gardens are already well documented by scholars, and the authors draw attention to source books and articles. Others have never previously been described, and these entries have required much original research. In all entries the authors are driven by the conviction that change in a garden is an expression of the state of mind, wealth and optimism of its owner and can only be understood in that context. Caroline Palmer, an anthropologist, and Penny David, a historian, have delved to expose not only the structure of each garden but the human stories that underlie its existence. Many other gardens await similar scrutiny. The Gazetteer compiled by geographer Ros Laidlaw includes map references to sites where significant gardens do, or did, exist.

Private Collection

A rare snapshot of gardening staff: head gardener T. Thomas and an unnamed assistant outside a glasshouse at Derry Ormond c. 1910.

The authors are to be congratulated on their painstaking work, and special thanks must be given to Michael Norman for acting as business manager and fund-raiser for the project.

It must be stressed that most of the gardens are in private hands and, unless stated otherwise, there is no automatic right of admission. However, certain private gardens do hold open days, and Hafod and Llanerchaeron offer regular access, allowing visitors to sample at least some of the historic parks and gardens of Ceredigion.

Donald Moore, Ceredigion Branch Chairman

Authors' Foreword:
Some Gardens Described

The gardens described in the following pages represent the tip of an iceberg whose hidden dimensions are yet to be revealed. We know of many more tantalizing facts around which fascinating stories could be woven – had we but space and time. There are documented gardens that have disappeared, like Peterwell ('four great towers crowned with domes' and 'the extraordinary flower garden and fruit trees which grew on its roof') or Foelallt, whose 'Park and Plantation of about 80 acres' and 'Lawn, Garden and Shrubbery' described in a mid 19th-century bill of sale were deliberately returned to farmland in the early 1900s. There are gardens still in existence where Augustus John painted and Dylan Thomas wrote, and where the model for Sebastian Flyte in *Brideshead Revisited* entertained his friends. These are among the ones that got away – but they deserve recognition.

What we have found so far is rewarding. Ceredigion has (or had) stove houses, icehouses, summerhouses, designed lodges, picturesque landscapes, exotic trees; a maze; bee boles; stew ponds, lakes, cold baths; the people who made these gardens include privateers, soldiers, sailors, lawyers, aesthetes and rakes. Often it was the wives and widows (and in one case the children!) who wielded the influence in garden design.

Harder to find out about are the people who actually did the gardening. Census returns record the occupation of 'gardener' and the county is dotted with gardener's cottages. People may remember that their grandfather was a gardener or their grandmother a maid, but photographs of working gardeners like those at Derry Ormond and Trawsgoed are rare and the subjects seldom named. Occasionally gardeners' notebooks recording planting plans, purchases and surpluses have survived, but for the most part only trees and structures commemorate their work. There is also little evidence of the humbler gardens. Until the advent of photography we are afforded few incidental glimpses of 'ordinary' private gardens.

The eleven sites star-rated in the *Register* are described here, but we admit to a touch of serendipity and of personal bias about the selection of the other twenty gardens. Some are included because members have explored and researched them in preparation for branch visits, to write articles for other publications or through personal curiosity. Others have been researched anew, and were selected as representative examples of their genre. There are, of course, many more country houses in the Teifi valley, or Victorian villas around Aberystwyth, equally deserving of attention.

The work of recording gardens is a continuing process, and descriptions must inevitably be revised as new information comes to light. The entries that follow are correct to the best of our knowledge at the time of publication, and any errors and the opinions expressed are our own. On the whole we have worked with information that is in the public domain. Some owners or former owners have been also been very helpful – and gratifyingly delighted when we have been able to tell them things that they did not already know. We record our gratitude to the many who have ferreted out old pictures or diaries for us to see, and welcomed us on our quest. We are also especially grateful to several scholars: Arthur Chater, who has unstintingly shared his expertise on the trees, Tom Lloyd and Michael Freeman who have contributed unpublished discoveries of their own and Donald Moore for his perceptive comments and scrupulous attention to detail.

Caroline Palmer, Penny David & Ros Laidlaw

Aberllolwyn

LLANYCHAEARN

This has been a house of substance since at least the early 17th century, and significant owners have included Erasmus Lloyd JP (1627–88), his son Hugh (1676–1732) who was High Sheriff in 1714, and Thomas Hughes (1697–1771), High Sheriff 1760, all of whom have substantial memorials in the parish church. These men predate the present house, which was probably built in the late 18th century at a time when it was home to Thomas Hughes's bachelor son Erasmus, his sister Mary and her husband Edward Hughes. It faces south-west and is set in a beechwood pleasure ground flanked to the west by the Aberystwyth–Aberaeron turnpike, and to the east by the wooded valley of Nant Llolwyn. Certainly it was built by the time Mrs Johnes of Hafod walked here from her temporary home at Castle Hill in 1809 to see 'that fine mansion' and the new heiress of Aberllolwyn, Elizabeth Jane Hughes of Morfa Bychan, who had startled the neighbourhood by her sudden marriage, aged 47, to widower John Bowen of Castle Green.

John Bowen died in 1815 and Elizabeth in 1818. Her estate passed to her brother and his descendants, none of whom resided at Aberllolwyn, but who extensively mortgaged it to other Cardiganshire landowners – George Jeffreys of Glandyfi and the Revd Lewis Charles Davies of Ynyshir.[1] It was leased to various gentlefolk for most of the 19th century. Cartographic information is furnished by the tithe survey of 1845 and by a 14-year lease of the house and 34 acres to Major Charles Richardes of the 8th Regiment of Bombay Native Infantry (brother of R. Richardes of Penglais and W.E. Richardes of Bryneithin) in 1846.[2] The tithe map probably derives from an earlier survey and shows the mansion approached from the turnpike by a curving drive through the plantation. Buildings are shown just south-east of the mansion (possibly remnants of the old house) and beyond them an enclosed garden with a glasshouse attached to its south-east-facing wall. The latter plan, being drawn by local surveyor George Pugh for the purpose of the lease, is a precise representation of what was there in 1846. The

Artist's impression of the house, on a plan of Aberllolwyn Estate prepared for an auction sale c. 1859.

buildings south-east of the mansion had been removed and entire area incorporated into the pleasure grounds which surrounded it. New outbuildings had been built against the west side of the walled garden, and the small field to the east was a paddock. The rest of the estate – the two substantial farms of Brynyrchain and Esgair-hir and land and houses at Rhydygwin and Chancery – totalling some 400 acres was separately let.

In 1859 the proprietor Thomas Hughes was declared bankrupt and died. A sale plan was prepared for the Aberllolwyn estate at about this time, but the complex of mortgages may have prevented the sale.[3] It is valuable for including the lithograph illustration of the house shown here, which gives a somewhat exaggerated impression of the mountain setting and also shows a square lodge with central chimney, very like the late 18th-century lodges at Llanerchaeron, Pontfaen Cottage and Clwyd Ddu. Unfortunately no map confirms the existence of this feature. The picture shows a mixed planting of deciduous and evergreen trees in the pleasure grounds and a ha-ha or railing separating the sundial, paths and informal flower beds of the garden from the grazing cattle in the field to the south.

The most memorably spendthrift tenant of Aberllolwyn was Mark John Tredwell, a young man of 21 with a fortune derived from his father Solomon Tredwell's endeavours in railway construction in Britain and India, who took a 21-year lease of the Aberllolwyn estate in 1878. He spent large sums of money on improvements to the house and garden, and hosted lavish garden parties (sometimes marred by rain) at Aberllolwyn. However, the most dramatic garden edifice associated with Aberllolwyn is not on the lands of the house but a crumble of rubble on an island at the south end of Llyn Eiddwen, 6 miles away on Mynydd Bach near Trefenter. Here at the source of the Aeron he employed local labour to erect a dry-stone wall around the island's circumference and built a folly tower and other buildings in which to host wild parties for his friends. Many were accommodated at the Queen's Hotel, Aberystwyth, and taken at Tredwell's expense by livery and then by boat to summer orgies in 1879. Even Tredwell's resources proved inadequate to this project and after an expensive lawsuit with his builder, he left Aberllolwyn after only four years. The disposal sale at Aberllolwyn in 1881 included huts built for guest accommodation, a great variety of exotic fowls, garden plants, a monkey and a bear. Tredwell eventually died, almost penniless, in London in 1930.[4]

The estate was eventually sold at auction in 1887[5] and the 25-inch OS survey of 1888 shows that there was, by then, a second, freestanding glasshouse or vinery in the walled garden and a fountain in front of the mansion.

Sketch of Tredwell's Castle by E.T. Price of Llanrhystud. NLW Drawing Vol. 171, p. 10.

The fishpond in Cae Mawr is also shown. The walks in the grounds took in the partially walled kitchen garden and the wooded valley of the Llolwyn. It was up for sale again in 1900, and this catalogue notes that the vendor, solicitor Griffith Jones, had in the previous 13 years planted costly and ornamental trees in the dingle.[6] Few noteworthy trees survive today. There is a London plane Platanus x hispanica where the stream joins the Ystwyth at Pont Llolwyn. The pleasure grounds contain mixed woodland, beech, Pinus nigra, and P. sylvestris and there is a Cedrus deodara near the house. Perhaps the most remarkable tree is the black poplar Populus nigra beside the pond, where it frames the view to the south-west. This is one of only 30 in the county, all of which are of the same male clone. It is quite distinct from the black poplars to be found on the Welsh borders, and implies a single origin by cuttings from an ancestral tree.   C.P.

[1] NLW MSS, Cwmere Deposit 20, 24, 25, 26, 27, 28, 29, 30.
[2] NLW Glanpaith MS 124.
[3] Plan of the Aberllolwyn Estate, lithographers M. & M.W. Lambert, Newcastle upon Tyne. NLW MS Gogerddan box 81. (Although undated, the identities of the named adjoining landowners fixes the date to 1854–60.)
[4] Phillips, R., 'The Castle on the lake' in Country Quest 16, 12, pp. 5-7 (1976).
[5] NLW Cards. Sale Catalogue 86.
[6] NLW Cards. Sale Catalogue 87.

Abermâd & Henblas

LLANYCHAEARN

The old Abermaide, 'standing on an arm of the Ystwyth' where it is joined by the Mâd, was formerly a part of the Ystrad Fflur grange of Strata Florida, and included, since at least 1533, a farmstead and, to the west, a corn mill in perilous range of flooding from the leat on which it stands. In the 16th century the somewhat lawless Lloyds of Abermâd destroyed the existing mill belonging to Thomas Pryse and re-used the millstones to build their own at this site.

By the time of the tithe survey of 1845, much of the Ystwyth valley land, including Abermâd, the mill and nearby Alltmai farm, was the property of the Earl of Lisburne. Abermâd was tenanted by Isaac Rowlands and consisted of a 367-acre farm situated on the boundary between Llanychaearn and Llanilar parishes. The mill and 11 acres was tenanted by Mary Jones. Abermâd (Abermaide as it was then known) was by now a stylish, boxy, three-storey Georgian residence adjoining the older homestead and stables and approached by a straight drive whose bifurcating intersection with the public road enclosed a small plantation. Two acres to the north-west of the house are described as orchard and garden.

Abermaide was bought in 1852 by Lewis Pugh, grandson of the substantial farmer Humphrey Pugh of Penygraig, Llanychaearn. On his death in 1868, his estate amounted to eleven farms in the Ystwyth valley, sheepwalks on Plynlimon, and three farms near Glandyfi: Cymerau, Dymin and Penrhyngerwyn. It was left to his nephew Lewis Pugh Evans of Lovesgrove on condition that he changed his name to Lewis Pugh Evans Pugh. Enriched by a successful career as a barrister in Calcutta, and a talent for gambling on the races, Lewis Pugh Evans Pugh and his wife Veronica Harriet were persuaded to commission J.P. Seddon (who was then working in Aberystwyth modifying his elaborate building, the uncompleted Castle House Hotel, for its new function as the University College of Wales) to build him a sumptuous residence, which Nicholas noted was under construction in 1870. The name was transferred to the new house, and the old one became known as Henblas (literally, the 'old place').

The reminiscences of Veronica Harriet Pugh give a colourful immediacy to this period. Seddon had grand plans, and 'It was difficult to bring his ideas down to ours. Finally we got the design for the house as it now stands.' Seddon incorporated pillars originally intended for the hotel in Aberystwyth, and many of the interior features and furnishings were designed by him or by a foreman or pupil of William Morris. The sitting rooms were papered with Morris designs selected by his followers the Misses

Henblas set amidst mature limes and beeches.

CDP 2004

Abermâd in the late 19th century.

Garrett. It all cost far more than expected. 'It was supposed to be £4,000 but Lewis Williams (our agent) always said nearer £20,000 altogether with stables and garden and grounds.' The house was completed in 1873, but the garden was already under way. Veronica Pugh was directly involved:

> We began the garden before the house. My old friend Mrs Pirie Gordon engaged Hutchinson and sent him down from Scotland before we knew it, so we had to give him a job! Splendid old fellow, and what a man for work....
>
> I got dreadful rheumatism in my knees about this time, planting out the ornamental shrubs between the house and the main gate. Hutchinson, splendid gardener though he was, could never do anything out of the diametric line and he would probably have made a chess board of it if I had not just gone and stood where nearly every tree and shrub was put in. The shrubs are now where the old farm buildings were, and well I remember watching the fowls being fed in the yard and the peacock and his harem.... They roosted in the big ash tree going down from the house to the garden and ravine. The tree grew below the path and a large branch spread across and over the path … About this time our Lewis planted the Wellingtonia at Tŷ issa in the middle of the new plantation – how I have watched it growing year by year little dreaming who would benefit from it.[1]

The garden to which she refers was down on the flood plain north-west of Henblas, and was a lavish Victorian brick structure entered through a tall pedimented arch of yellow and red brick. On the south-facing walls was an extensive L-shaped range of very tall glasshouses and a central projecting conservatory with underfloor heating. The exterior of these walls is insulated by an L-shaped range of outbuildings. A roadside lodge and extensive stable courtyard beside Afon Fâd completed the aggrandizement of Abermâd.

Lewis and Veronica did not end their days at Abermâd, for a disastrous investment in the South Wales coal industry precipitated the sale of Abermaide in 1906, and the Pughs moved to Cymerau, and built a more modest new house near the disused Cardiganshire Slate Works. Further financial difficulties sent Lewis Pugh back to India, where he died in 1908.

The most distinctive feature of the grounds of Abermâd and Henblas are the large wellingtonias *Sequoiadendron giganteum* in the grounds and fields nearby and the hybrid limes which margin the road. There are also a number of large Douglas firs *Pseudotsuga menziesii* and one *Cedrus deodara* south-east of the mansion, and a single silver fir *Abies alba* to the west. A curious feature of the planting around the mansion is the presence of two pairs of twinned trees, in which dissimilar trees planted in the same hole have, in the course of their growth, fused together. South of the mansion an ash and a sycamore of similar size and girth are fused together, while to the north-west two different oaks, *Quercus petraea* and *Q. x turneri* are similarly conjoined.[2] The mansion and its separate stable block are set in shrubberies of cherry laurel. Since 1948 Abermâd has served successively as prep school and residential nursing home and its grounds have been tidily maintained.   *C.P.*

[1] Journal of Veronica Harriet Pugh (private coll. Mrs Joy Neal)
[2] A.O. Chater pers. comm.

Alltyrodyn, Galltyrodyn

LLANDYSUL

The Afon Cletwr flows south through a narrow valley to join the Teifi east of Llandysul. Alltyrodyn Hall and home farm, and the core of its pleasure grounds, occupy a terrace along the contours of the west-facing slope almost 3 miles upriver, in a sheltered site with modest, handsome views. The present estate makes an elongated arc downhill from the B4459. History records ownership by the ubiquitous Lloyds of south Ceredigion, noting particularly the Royalist David Lloyd who had to compound for his delinquency in 1648, and a fine genealogical library that drew and impressed visitors around 1800. The property was apparently aesthetically undistinguished until sometime between 1820 and 1840, when a vast rebuilding project transformed the house and its surroundings into an elegant Regency period piece.

PD 2004

Specific allusions to early garden interest at Alltyrodyn form part of the content of a letter dated 4 May 1744 from one David Lloyd (possibly 1724–79?) to an unidentified 'Dear Madam' – one of those rare glimpses into past gardens preserved as if in amber, luminous but detached. The letter begins, 'Does my dear delight in gardens? O! How I can anticipate the pleasures we shall enjoy', and goes on to mention his satisfaction in his beans, cauliflowers and cucumbers. The writer boasts of his delicious arbours, wide canals and melonry ('it is a nonpareil!').[1] He knows his horticulture, but the overall tone of this substantial letter is that of an ardent wooer, and his garden descriptions and vegetable allusions should be seen in the context of the vigorous allegorical prose of the 18th century.

The simple, classical design of the three-storey house (grade II★) is reminiscent of John Nash, and the fine service courtyard behind it bears a strong similarity to Llanerchaeron's,[2] although if Alltyrodyn was remodelled in imitation of Llanerchaeron, one would expect this to have been done in the very early 1800s. Both dating and motivation are obscure: the OS 1st Edition map of 1830 shows a house in the present position with a different set of outbuildings, but detail in this one-inch scale is hard to decipher. The Alltyrodyn genealogy of the early 19th century is also often confused.

Two inscribed dates offer clues. A date-stone of 1830 in the kitchen garden and a plaque dated 1840 in the stable courtyard commemorate John Lloyd Esq. Known as 'Lloyd Coch' or 'Lloyd the Red',[3] John (1803–41) was the younger son of David Lloyd (1738–1822), High Sheriff in 1780, and of Elizabeth Evans of Highmead (1770–1805). All three have monuments in Llandysul parish church. That to David Lloyd commemorating his 'benevolence, integrity, and great mental attainments' was erected by his widow, Caroline Lloyd (née Russell);[4] further information regarding this second wife could help shed light on a period when new building might have been in the planning.

Fenton (1804–13) and Malkin (1807) both visited Alltyrodyn, commenting on the setting rather than a new house. Fenton mentioned the 'tumulus' of Tomen Rhyd Owen, which had been planted with silver fir Abies alba. Meyrick (1810) was interested in pedigree rather than topography, and recorded three surviving children, Anne, David and John.

Perhaps it was the death of the older brother David in the 1820s that spurred John Lloyd to expend his unexpected inheritance on improvements. (He also controversially built a Unitarian chapel dedicated to St David in 1835.[5]) One oblique footnote to John Lloyd's gardening activity has surfaced in the correspondence of his kinsmen. Somehow the owner of this model house and garden was saddled with a most unsatisfactory employee: 'Of all sulky brutes that ever I came across Will the gardener is the greatest,' wrote D.H. Glyn of Llwynhelig (Carms.) to his uncle Herbert Evans of Highmead; later, with Will preparing to return to Alltyrodyn in March 1837, Glyn reported that 'Lloyd says distress makes him take him back'.[6]

John Lloyd seems to have been the creator of the handsome farm buildings and the gardens. We can still admire the bones of the pleasure grounds – two entrance drives with lodges (South Lodge, listed grade II, is absent from the 1841 tithe map and was probably built by John Lloyd-Davies); plus walks amid woods that still contain fine trees including mature limes, beeches, a wellingtonia and a large noble fir *Abies procera* (girth 351cm) that must have been planted soon after its introduction to Britain from north-west America in 1830.

The layout used the terrain to advantage. The steep slope behind the house is laced with woodland walks leading to a wooden summerhouse which replaces an original building. The level platform on which the house stands has lawned formal gardens to the south. The centrepiece of the oval forecourt, now a brick-edged flower bed, was originally a fountain. Beyond, on axis from the front door, were two flights of steps leading over a ha-ha to a path across the field below to a bridge over the Cletwr. (The bridge is gone but its site is marked today by a Scots pine, a cedar of Lebanon and one of only three incense cedars *Calocedrus decurrens* in Ceredigion.) A further path leading to a gazebo perhaps constituted 'the grounds on the opposite side of the river … tastefully and judiciously laid out' described in Lewis (1842 edition). The visit took place during John Lloyd's incumbency, recording 'an elegant modern mansion' and the 'thriving plantation' that enclosed it.

Near the south entrance the Afon Geyron passes under the B4459 to flow through a small dammed pond between two series of ornamental cascades. Stone-edged paths wander through a shrubbery of rhododendron and laurel under beech, oak and sycamore. Another pond makes a separate water feature in a grove of trees to the north-east of the house, near the flower garden.

John Lloyd was also presumably responsible for the two walled gardens. The large kitchen

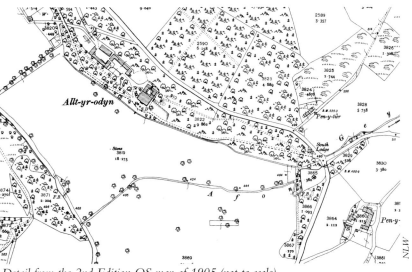

Detail from the 2nd Edition OS map of 1905 (not to scale).

garden retains traces of perimeter and cruciform paths and the footings of former glasshouses and boiler house. Garden Cottage (grade II) is built against the north wall of the kitchen garden. Next door, nearer the house, is an irregular five-sided flower garden with central dipping pool. But a handful of more unusual features survives at Alltyrodyn.

Access between house and service areas was delicately managed. Servants walked between walled gardens and domestic quarters via a sunken path (and visited a lavatory well below ground level). The north drive crossed a farm track over a single-arch stone bridge as it approached the house. Near this bridge is a two-roomed building with gothic windows, now roofless, housing a spring-fed cold bath. Tucked into a south-facing corner beyond the kitchen and flower gardens lie the remains of that Ceredigion rarity, an orangery, overlooking the valley.

On 10 September 1841 John Lloyd died childless ('who in life was beloved and in death is deeply lamented by a numerous circle of friends' noted the *Carmarthen Journal*). His wife Dorothy Alicia Lloyd had died aged 30 in 1837. The tithe schedule of 31 December 1841 already noted the owner as John Lloyd-Davies (1801–60) of nearby Blaendyffryn in Bangor Teifi parish, High Sheriff in 1845, who in 1825 had married Anne (1794–1853).[7] Heirs to the joined estates in the next two generations – Arthur Lloyd-Davies (1827–52) and John Davies-Lloyd (1850–78) – were short-lived, and horticultural development as a consequence unremarkable, although repairs and renovations recorded between 1872 and 1878 on the Alltyrodyn and Blaendyffryn estates included planting 189,000 trees at an outlay of £318.[8]

Around 1881 the estate was purchased by the Stewarts, who lived there until 1929 and sold the property in 1947. To their incumbency dates the list of plants grown at

Alltyrodyn: interior of the gothic-style cold bath.

PD 2004

Alltyrodyn recorded in a publication of 1896.[9] Mr Morris the gardener is credited as the source of information, and the plants are classified as greenhouse or hardy flowers, trees, vegetables and shrubs. The large number of ferns in the 'flowers' category suggests there may have been a fern house.

The present owners maintain the pleasure grounds, dealing with the ravages of time - silting ponds, breached dams and superannuated trees. They regularly admit the public to the garden as part of the National Gardens Scheme. Despite the fact that a tennis court had appeared by the 1920s – and 'adjoining it a tastefully designed DUTCH GARDEN approached by steps with stone piers'[10] – today the one major intrusion into the integrity of the Regency layout is a garden enclosure at the far end of the lawned platform to the south of the house – a memorial to Alick Stewart, killed aged 21 at Ypres in 1915.   *P.D.*

[1] Baker-Jones, Leslie (1999) p. 108. NLW Ms 8724B.

[2] Cadw/ICOMOS, *Register.*

[3] Eyre Evans (1903) p. 163.

[4] Theakston, Lucy E. Lloyd, *Some family records and pedigrees of the Lloyds of Allt yr Odyn &c*, Oxford, 1913.

[5] Eyre Evans (1903) p. 166.

[6] NLW Highmead papers 2394 & 2397.

[7] This was the widowed Anne Stewart, daughter of John, younger brother of David Lloyd (1738–1822), and cousin of the John Lloyd who was active in the 1830s .

[8] Baker-Jones, Leslie (1999) p. 81. NLW Ms 9871 C

[9] Davies, W.J., *Hanes Plwyf Llandyssul*, 1896, Gomer.

[10] Jackson Stops sale catalogue, 11 June 1929, Carmarthen Record Office.

Blaenpant
LLANDYGWYDD

Like Mary Ashby Lewis at Llanerchaeron, Maria Brigstocke of Blaenpant may be a childless footnote in the family lineage, but she was a most influential individual in the history of her home. As widow of independent means she exercised sole control over the ostentatious aggrandizement of the Blaenpant estate which took place from her husband's death in 1861 until her own in 1898.

Blaenpant has a distinguished history, having been in the 17th century a house of seven hearths, home of John Parry, High Sheriff of Cardiganshire in 1621. In the 18th century the marriage of the heiress Elizabeth Jenkins brought the estate to William Brigstocke of Llechdwny whose descendants were to own it for seven generations. Although the Brigstockes claim descent from Edward I, this branch of the family derived from a Croydon brewer, but by the mid 18th century they had become Cardiganshire lawyers and intelligentsia, and Blaenpant housed the famous antiquarian library of Sir Thomas Browne.

An estate survey for Blaenpant has yet to be discovered, so the first clear indication of its landscape comes from the tithe survey of 1839. The mansion owned almost half the parish of Llandygwydd, thirteen tenant farms and thirteen smallholdings totalling 2470 acres.

Brigstocke of Blaenpant also owned much land, and had mining interests at Kidwelly. Their house was by now a handsome mid 18th-century pedimented stone building overlooking a pleasure ground and ornamental pond, and embosomed, as several

The lakeside garden at Blaenpant in the late 19th century.

Private Collection

contemporary authors noted, in woods of stately growth and flourishing plantations.[1] The adjoining walled garden and home farm were also architecturally distinguished, and their agriculture 'uniformly good'.

The squire who inherited in 1831 was William Owen Brigstocke, aged 46, the eldest of eight children. His wife Maria was 22 years his junior and thus when he died aged 76 in 1861, she survived him for 37 years. These were years which saw the engineering of a very substantial lake at the top of the wooded dingle. Across this lake was built a two-arched bridge which carried the new carriage drive across the water, allowing a prospect of the best elevation of the house on the route to the elegant coach house north-east of the house.

Further down the dingle a Swiss Cottage was built in the quarry, and was occupied by estate workers, the gardener Daniel Jones and his family, in 1871. Both the Swiss Cottage and the ornamental bridge had a distinctive timbered style which is recorded in the photographs taken by local photographer Tom Mathias of Cilgerran in the late 19th century. During this period the public road which approaches

Blaenpant: the Swiss Cottage in the dingle. Photographer Tom Mathias of Cilgerran (1866–1940).

Llandygwydd from the north was moved westward, enlarging the pleasure grounds south-west of Blaenpant and leaving an avenue of trees crossing an open field. An avenue forming a south-easterly axis from the house was also abandoned.

Maria Brigstocke is remembered as a powerful old lady in south Cardiganshire, whose influence was widespread. There are some accounts indicating that she sought to control the voting choices of her tenantry, and that tenants who failed to co-operate were evicted.[2] However she is also remembered as a kind-hearted and noble old lady, who 'under her rugged exterior and brusqueness of manner possessed a kind heart' and took a lifelong interest in the welfare of her tenants. She had the church at Llandygwydd erected in 1853 as her chapel of ease. Exceptionally, this church was deconsecrated and pulled down in 2000.

Blaenpant fared little better, its lake empty and bridge dilapidated, gardens overgrown and a large portion of the house demolished in the late 20th century.

Most of the fine trees have gone, to be succeeded by natural regeneration, chiefly of sycamores, near the mansion or by plantations of conifers in the dingle. There are a few interesting survivors: particularly three fine specimens of Dutch elm

The bridge over the lake in the early 1900s. Photographer Tom Mathias.

Ulmus x *hollandica* and one wych elm *U. glabra* which, despite diseased and suckering English elm *U. procera* near by, have remained healthy. Two large field maples *Acer campestre* adjoin the drive south-west of the house, and another stands near the north end of the now ruined bridge over the lake. A very large spreading copper beech (possibly the largest in Ceredigion) and some interesting hybrid rhododendrons are south of the lake, while four similar-sized *Acer palmatum* at its north-west end are perhaps remnants of the Japanese garden seen in a late 19th-century photograph. English and Irish yews west of the house demark former paths and driveways. A single lime *Tilia* x *europaea* stands south-east of the mansion. The former avenue crossing the field north-east of the mansion was also of limes, but of these, just one recently killed tree remains.

The dilapidation at the mansion has now been halted and the Swiss Cottage has also been renovated and enlarged by its owners. The walled kitchen gardens survive, with the remnants of some fine Victorian heated greenhouses. As at other prestigious early 19th-century walled gardens, the south-facing fruit walls are lined with brick. They are locally remarkable for the inclusion of unusual L-shaped bonding bricks, which are also found in the walled gardens of Glanhelig, Llechryd, another mansion owned by a branch of the Brigstocke family. Externally to the garden, on the south-west and north-west sides, is an additional L-shaped enclosure margined by a distinctive fence of large upright slabs of Cilgerran slate linked together by iron cramps. This arrangement is apparent on the tithe survey, with a further fenced area outside it.

There is documentary evidence of an icehouse at Blaenpant. It was unusual in being a budget design, in which the pit was lined not with stone, but with a tapering wooden frame lined with an insulating layer of vertically arranged wheat straw. The space between the

CDP 2003

Part of the interior of the brick-lined walled garden.

earth walls and the frame was packed with brushwood and tree branches and the roof was composed of 2–3 feet of thatch.[3] A letter and plan reveal that it cost just £12–£15 to build, in contrast to a masonry icehouse which could cost £200–£300.

Its component parts all being biodegradable, the icehouse does not survive except as a deep hole in the ground just south of the now ruined South Lodge in the dingle.   *C.P.*

[1] Meyrick (1810), Carlisle (1811), Lewis (1849).
[2] *Cardiganshire and Teivyside Advertiser* 1910, 14 January, 21 January.
[3] Carmarthen Record Office. Cawdor box 169

Bronpadarn
LLANBADARN FAWR

Bronpadarn is approached from the steep slope up Primrose Hill, which rises from the ancient church at the centre of Llanbadarn village. It represents a later development in the social history of Aberystwyth when lavish gardens and glasshouses were no longer the preserve of the landed gentry. Capt. George Weir Cosens, a retired officer of the 85th Light Infantry, was no local landowner, but first appears in the area in the census of 1871 as a 30-year-old married man with three infant children and a wife and widowed mother-in-law. All were Scottish-born so it is not obvious what drew them to the area. He rented Ynyshir mansion, and later Cwmcynfelin mansion from the trustees of that estate, and then bought two acres of land on Primrose Hill. Here in the mid 1880s he erected Bronpadarn, a fashionable stone mansion, with an attached conservatory and adjoining coach house and stables. His was the first house in Llanbadarn to be connected, in 1888, to the new Aberystwyth Corporation reservoir near by.

Several other comparable villas – Cwm Padarn, Fronfraith and Nantceirio – were built at this time, but none matched Bronpadarn for the style and quality of its garden, with its exotic plantings of trees and shrubs and no less than five glasshouses all situated in the polite areas of the grounds and probably devoted to flowers and exotic fruit.

Three large interconnected glasshouses faced south-west across the dingle and were approached by slate steps rising to a central door. A fourth, exceptionally tall, greenhouse was attached to the south-east face of the stables. The setting of these glasshouses was in grass, with chusan palms *Trachycarpus fortunei*, Japanese acers, and ginkgo planted near by. Below, Cwm Padarn dingle was planted with ginkgos, yews, lime, copper beech and cedar of Lebanon, and underplanted with Victorian evergreens: bamboo, cherry laurel, Portugal laurel, Highclere holly and *Viburnum tinus*. The stream had been excavated to form a gorge and a substantial pool.

Along the upper margin of the garden is a very substantial raised walk, which runs the full width of the plot, from Primrose Hill to Penygraig Lane. This gave the garden a magnificent panoramic view out over the Rheidol valley towards Pendinas. It was accessible only from within the garden, and included along its length a walk-through glasshouse. Below it was the largely oriental planting near the house, various Japanese acers, magnolias, ginkgo, chusan palms, and the rare Hinoki cypress *Chamaecyparis obtusa* 'Filicoides'. Below the entrance drive was an orchard and a two-roomed summerhouse. West of the orchard, on the edge of the dingle, is a very fine group of smooth-leaved elm *Ulmus carpinifolia*.

The quality of this garden was still outstanding in the early 20th century when those of many gentry mansions were suffering neglect. In 1917 it was one of just twelve listed in Cardiganshire in the *Gardeners' Chronicle, Horticultural Directory and Yearbook*. It was then the home of Major L.J. Mathias, CBE, JP, DL, senior partner in the shipowning firm of J. Mathias and Sons, and an influential figure in local affairs. Later it became the private residence of the Principal of the Welsh College of Librarianship, and then fell into institutional use. Recent restoration and conversion of the mansion has been accompanied by the building of new houses in the garden, but many traces of its Victorian splendour remain, and the former private path along the side of the dingle is now used as a public right of way.   *C.P.*

Bryneithin
LLANYCHAEARN

The garden at Bryneithin sits at the heart of a radial pattern of fields enclosing about 53 acres of land on high ground close to the coast south of Aberystwyth. At the centre is a more or less circular walled enclosure of just less than two acres and within this enclosure is the present house and farmstead. It has been suggested that this arrangement is an archaeological remnant of a medieval *trefgordd* or family holding of land.[1]

Until the 19th century this holding was known as Tynygwndwn and contained a farmhouse, which was not deemed significant by the cartographers who surveyed for the first Ordnance Survey in 1820. It was bought in 1820 from Roderick Richardes of Penglais by his younger brother William Eardley Richardes (born 1794), who had served with the Royal Artillery in the Campaign of 1814–15, and in the army of occupation after Waterloo. Richardes remodelled and enlarged the house, adding on to the east side a one-storey suite of

CDP 2004

The Wellington monument on Pendinas.

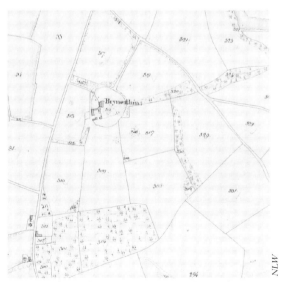

NLW

A detail of the tithe map (1845) shows the circular homestead. Radial fields were named after military ranks.

rooms with gothic windows and ornate veranda in the Strawberry Hill gothic style. It was now known as Bryneithin (literally Gorse Hill) and is designated a gentleman's seat in the 1-inch OS map published in 1834. Interestingly, in 1832 it was the residence from which Emma Davies, daughter of John Davies of Strawberry Hill, married Matthew Davies of Tanybwlch. This suggests that the homage to Horace Walpole's residence at Twickenham may be more than coincidental.

Richardes built the massive perimeter walls which are up to 15ft tall at the gateway, and the round tower gazebo on to the north wall. The visitor climbed an external stair of protruding slates to enter a circular room at the top of the tower and look out through a window framing the view northward towards Pendinas, the town of Aberystwyth and the sea.

It was also W.E. Richardes who arranged the construction in 1856 of the Wellington monument on top of Pendinas. The principal arable fields around the house were also renamed by this military enthusiast. They are labelled on the tithe schedule, in clockwise order, as General, Governor, Captain, Lieutenant and Major. Most have marginal or corner plantations of trees planted with aesthetic intent to give a more gentrified appearance to the farm. Richardes remained at Bryneithin until his death aged 80 in 1874.

A stream enters the walled garden through a brick arched culvert and supplies a pond system within the walls. There are orchard trees within the walled garden, and also in a subsidiary walled orchard entered through a door in the east side of the garden wall. In the early 20th century a lodge was built on the approach from the north-east. In 1944 Bryneithin became the home of the prominent Welsh language campaigner and founder of the Urdd Gobaith Cymru youth movement, Ifan ab Owen Edwards. *C.P.*

[1] Davies, J.L. & Kirby, D.P.,(eds.) *Cardiganshire County History*, Vol. I, Cardiff, 1994.

Bryneithin in 1896, from an album belonging to Lizzie Richardes of Bryneithin (née Davies of Ffosrhydgaled). NLW Photo album 297.

Castle Green
CARDIGAN ST MARY

Castle Green is situated within the ruins of a medieval castle. Cardigan castle was built by the Normans on a strategic eminence overlooking a ford on the river Teifi, not far from the sea. It witnessed a turbulent history, and it is also famous as the venue of the first recorded Welsh *eisteddfod*, held there in 1176 by the Lord Rhys. Successively damaged by siege and rebuilt, it last discharged a military function as a Royalist stronghold in the Civil War. Subsequently its stone was pillaged for other buildings, and it became a dilapidated ruin, though the town of Cardigan continued to use parts of the building for administration and as a prison. In 1713 the ground within the castle was landscaped to provide a bowling green devised by the then mayor, Lewis Price. From then on it became known as Castle Green.

This piece of public land, set about with crumbling walls and towers matted with ivy, was sold to a private owner in 1785, and in 1805 was acquired by attorney John Bowen of Cardigan Priory, who built a Georgian house on the site of the keep, integrating parts of the building into his cellar. Carlisle in 1811 recorded that Bowen had lowered the curtain wall between the two surviving towers, and sloped the green down 'so as to form a hanging garden'. The immensely spreading Turkey oak *Quercus cerris* (girth 374cm) which stands today at the top of this slope may date from Bowen's landscaping efforts. The work may have been barely completed when he died in 1815 but his contribution was not forgotten. Samuel Lewis in 1832 described how the outer ward had been 'converted into a verdant lawn, tastefully disposed in pastures, the whole effected by John Bowen Esq'.

The distinctive character of Castle Green house today derives from its next owner, Arthur Jones (High Sheriff 1827), who employed Daniel and John Evans of Eglwyswrw to put on a new Regency façade and an additional wing. A separate gardener's house was built to the north, and a range of stables and accommodation at the bottom of the slope. In 1836 Castle Green was bought by the merchant David Davies (mayor of Cardigan 1844) and passed to his descendants, till it was sold in 1923 to Cardigan auctioneer John Evans (mayor of Cardigan 1932). Its most recent owner, Barbara Woods, who occupied Castle Green from 1940 to 1996, presided over its decline from elegant mansion to overgrown ruin.

The OS 25-inch map of 1888 and late 19th-

Castle Green depicted in Nicholas (1872).

Castle Green: the neglected house and garden in 1988.

© G. K. Johnson

century photographs give the best indication of the garden within the castle. A productive vegetable garden, not walled, but divided by gravelled paths, lay to the north of the house. The space within the castle walls was landscaped with a perimeter path, viewing points from within the parapet, and plantings of evergreen shrubs and informal borders. There were two lean-to greenhouses in the polite area inside the south-east facing wall on the approach to the house, one of which is remembered as a fernery. The house façade itself was ornamented with trelliswork.

The 19th-century plantings around the mansion include a copper beech and a common beech south of the mansion, a holm oak, ash and sycamore. Conifers *Cedrus deodara* and wellingtonia have not flourished on this site. Overgrown plants from the former shrubberies also reflect the Victorian enthusiasm for evergreens: yew, Highclere holly, spotted laurel, garden privet, cherry laurel, *Rhododendron ponticum*, *Lonicera nitida*, *Euonymus japonicus*, butcher's broom and snowberry.

Cardigan Castle has recently been acquired by Ceredigion County Council and conservation plans are being drawn up. The Regency domestic building and garden within the walls is, as much as the ancient castle ruins, a priority for conservation. *C.P.*

Also see: Johnson, G. K., *Castle in Crisis,* Cardigan 2002.

Castle Hill

LLANILAR

This trim mansion below the old motte and bailey castle was built in 1777 by John Williams in a situation close to the home of his married sister Elizabeth Parry at Llidiardau. An L-shaped tract of woodland links the two properties. However, John Williams died in 1806, whilst his son John Nathaniel Williams was still a minor. This made the house available to be leased in 1807 by the deeply disgruntled Thomas Johnes of Hafod whilst his own fire-wrecked mansion was being rebuilt. For his daughter Mariamne it must have been a pleasure to live just a short distance down the road from the three unmarried Parry girls, Elizabetha, Sarah and Penelope, at Llidiardau, and both she and her mother found it a very happy time. Thomas Johnes, however, was depressed, and as Mariamne remarked wryly in a letter, her father 'takes no pleasure in any situation which does not actually belong to him – which appears to me singular, for to me every place that is beautiful affords me the same delight as if I had an actual concern in it.' Three years later, Hafod having been rebuilt, the Johnes family went home.

John Nathaniel Williams married Sarah Elizabeth Loxdale of Shrewsbury, but predeceased her. She was the owner-occupier at the time of the tithe survey in 1845. The three-storey Georgian house looked out northward to Llanilar village from above a ha-ha. Beyond it spread a flat park or lawn of 38 acres on the floor of the Ystwyth valley. This was divided by water into three compartments: that nearest the mansion forming a triangular apron below the house, margined by ditches on three sides, to display grazing animals to best advantage. The polite approach to the mansion was via a low lodge on the Trawsgoed road, and passed through screening woodland before

emerging to the east of the house. This is probably the wood to which Meyrick refers in remarking that Williams had 'planted forest trees and firs to a very large amount'. The grounds immediately south of the mansion were described as a flower garden, whilst vegetables and fruit would have come from the distinctively curved walled kitchen garden on the far side of the road leading to the home farm.

Sarah had no issue, so the estate passed to her brother James Loxdale and has continued to pass, though rarely from father to son, down the Loxdale family ever since. In the mid 19th century alterations were made to the east end of the house, adding a two-storey wing with a belltower to summon the estate workers. By the late 19th century the 25-inch OS map shows several small glasshouses or frames and a well in the kitchen garden. There are some important ornamental trees close to the house including English yews in the former flower garden, a large cedar of Lebanon and a shapely tulip tree *Liriodendron tulipifera*.   *C.P.*

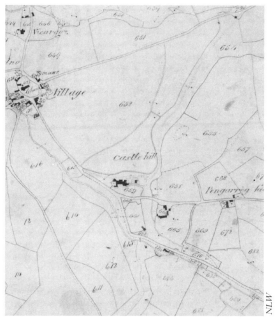

Detail of the tithe map (1845).

Cilgwyn
LLANDYFRÏOG

Twelve miles inland from Cardigan the Teifi river takes a contorted course around the rocky outcrop of Newcastle Emlyn castle and the old town clustered at its foot. Carmarthenshire begins south of the Teifi, while the high ground of south Cardiganshire rises to the north, dissected by deep wooded dingles. Cilgwyn is on the first of these dingles to the east of Newcastle Emlyn. The Cilgwyn estate once embraced vast acreages of land in Cardiganshire and Carmarthenshire, and large areas of the town of Llandysul. It had, since the 17th century, been the seat of the influential Lloyd family.

There used to be an old fortified Welsh house at Cilgwyn. While the Lloyds are well represented in wills and deeds, few visual clues remain. There are no known images of the old house and the Cilgwyn estate map of 1773, deposited in the National Library of Wales, is no longer to be found. Some of the oaks on the south-facing slopes above Newcastle Emlyn are of sufficient antiquity to date back to the 17th

Emlyn Cottage. Watercolour print, 19th century.

century, but for the most part the landscape today represents the influence of newer owners – some extremely new brooms sweeping clean.

This dramatic change in ownership was brought about by the will of Admiral Thomas Lloyd, who died in 1801. In partnership with Richard Brathwaite he had been owner of a privateer, and when this ship foundered off what is now known as Hall Island, Jamaica, the two men had tossed for the responsibility of selling landed property to make up losses and buy a new ship. Brathwaite lost the bet and sold property at Plymouth. Lloyd, the winner, is said to have been motivated to set the inequality straight, and left two-thirds of his very large estates to his erstwhile partner, now Admiral Brathwaite, his wife and their daughters and heirs. The consternation in the Teifi valley and particularly amongst the Lloyds of Coedmore, who received just a one-third share rather than the whole, was considerable.

Brathwaite never lived at Cilgwyn, and the partition of the land was not completed until 1833. However, by 1838, Brathwaite's daughter Jane Maria and son-in-law Benjamin Edward Hall were the landowners, and their eldest son Edward Crompton Lloyd Hall resided at Emlyn Cottage, a picturesque property by John Nash, which overlooked the Teifi and Newcastle Emlyn. Adjoining it was Adpar Hill, a three-storey boxy Georgian

Adpar Hill. Watercolour, 19th century.

house similar to Henblas, Abermâd, situated close to the road descending the hill from Ffostrasol to the bridge at Newcastle Emlyn. Adpar Hill was tenanted by John Beynon, a lawyer and businessman extremely active in the Turnpike Trust, and the old house at Cilgwyn was occupied by a surgeon, David Lewis.

Benjamin Hall died in 1849 and while the Cilgwyn estate was entailed upon his eldest son, his other property in Paddington, London, was divided between his three sons. This so enraged Edward Crompton Lloyd Hall that,

Cilgwyn. Photo by John Thomas, c. 1885.

although he accepted his inheritance, he rejected the family name, and adopted the surname of a putative ancestor – Fitzwilliam.[1]

In 1855 debts arising from his involvement in the Great Western Railway forced the family to flee to France to avoid the bailiffs, and it was ten years before he returned to take up residence at Adpar Hill.[2] He now set in train a major redevelopment of his inheritance: the demolition of Emlyn Cottage and construction of a new mansion on the site. He visited the Paris Exposition Universelle of 1878 and purchased from it a fine exhibition piece, a massive double-return staircase with fluted columns, all carved in French oak.[3] The new house had to be designed to accommodate this massive centrepiece. It was also to be supplied with all the latest conveniences: coal-fired central heating, and electricity generated by a water wheel in the factory beside the Teifi. E.C.L. Hall died in 1880, before his vision was enacted, while still residing at Adpar Hill. The first and most dynamic occupant was thus his son, Charles Home Lloyd Fitzwilliam, who

completed the transformation, moving into his new home, Cilgwyn, in 1887, and later demolishing neighbouring Adpar Hill, to avoid the risk of allowing poor relations to lodge so close by. Undoubtedly he was responsible for rearranging the layout of the eastern approach, building the two distinctive lodges which straddle the approaches, the stables, the battery house which housed the electricity-storage batteries, and for planting a variety of fashionable Victorian conifers around the house. He also razed the old house of Cilgwyn to the ground, and built a long barn there in its stead.

His son Col. Edward Crawford Lloyd Fitzwilliam inherited in 1928 and in the eight years before he died made a rare inter-war garden of linked ponds and choice rhododendrons in the dingle which drains south from Old Cilgwyn. A branch from the drive to the new mansion already led up the west side of the dingle. Now it was planted with an avenue of horse chestnuts. As fortunes of the 20th century beleaguered so many

25

Massive epicormic growth on the bole of a hybrid lime on the west lawn of Cilgwyn.

CDP 2004

owners of big houses, his son, Capt. Collinsplatt Lloyd Fitzwilliam, returned after its wartime requisitioning, not to the mansion, but to a small cottage which stood south of the former Old Cilgwyn. In the last 20 years this has been enlarged to a comfortable home by the fifth generation, Edward A. L. Fitzwilliam. The Victorian Cilgwyn, meanwhile, is now in separate ownership and in serious need of investment. It still has a handsome tall conservatory with fountain attached to the east side of the house, but the loss of the porch, the verandas, and the tower has much altered the appearance of the building.

The site thus reveals some traces of each phase, including a palimpsest of the gardens of Adpar Hill and Emlyn Cottage. The former is just a platform, set about with mature beeches and a few Scots pines. The garden cottage which faces on to the main road formerly belonged to Adpar Hill and is adjoined by the remains of a very large sweet chestnut. Behind it the extensive wooded Victorian garden with

walks and lawns has disappeared. Around Cilgwyn, east and west of the house, are traces of what may be Emlyn Cottage plantings: mature limes *Tilia* x *vulgaris* with massive growths of epicormic sprouts clothing their trunks, some venerable beeches, and two oaks symmetrically placed adjoining the south corners of the walled garden. There is also a very ancient multi-stemmed and collapsed *Laburnum anagyroides* on the edge of the lawn. The modest stone-built square vegetable garden with symmetrical crosspaths and stone lintels to its doorways seems to have been the walled garden of Emlyn Cottage; it appears on the tithe map of 1838. It lacks the brick-lined fruit walls or flue walls of more ostentatious Georgian walled gardens. Subsequent alterations in the late 19th century introduced additional entrances with brick lintels, and a small hot-water-pipe greenhouse on the inside of the north wall, with a boiler in the potting-shed on the other side.

Charles Home Lloyd Fitzwilliam's conifer planting incudes three Atlantic cedars which now partially block the view out over Newcastle Emlyn, and Douglas firs, Caucasian firs *Abies nordmanniana* and wellingtonias. Close to the house were a specimen larch, a *Cryptomeria japonica* and, until recently, a monkey puzzle. Four wellingtonias extend up the dingle towards Old Cilgwyn, and there is also the unexpected presence of a single *Abies alba* and a lone tulip tree *Liriodendron tulipifera* part way up the dingle beside the stream. Beside the easterly South Lodge are a very large *Chamaecyparis pisifera* 'Squarrosa' and a larch *Larix decidua* both with girths in excess of 220cm. The specimen larch on the lawn west of Cilgwyn is the hybrid Dunkeld larch *Larix* x *eurolepis*. This is a large tree (girth 200cm) but cannot be older than 100 years, for the hybrid was first noticed in Perthshire in 1904.[4] It does indicate an enthusiasm for new cultivars on the part of Fitzwilliam or his son, as does the

CDP 1996

The three-way concrete bridge across one of Col. E.C.L. Fitzwilliam's ponds at Old Cilgwyn.

considerable variety of unusual holly cultivars in the shrubbery beside the house.

Col. Edward Crawford Lloyd Fitzwilliam's ponds included a most unusual cast-concrete three-way bridge traversing the middle pond. He is said to have purchased a great quantity of rhododendrons from the Chelsea Flower Show in 1924. Certainly the landscaping of the dingle with a network of paths edged with cherry laurel probably dates from this time. This planting has become impenetrable and is being cleared. Many of the original rhododendrons, grafted on to *Rhododendron ponticum* stock, have since reverted to species but some, such as a very large *R.* 'Cynthia' remain.

It is a pleasing symmetry that Edward Fitzwilliam is an extremely knowledgeable rhododendron gardener who is reclaiming his grandfather's garden in the dingle, and restoring the ponds. Old Cilgwyn, a predominantly modern stone house, stands in a magnificent garden which is regularly opened to the public under the NGS. Of the original Cilgwyn of the Lloyds, there is no longer any trace.   *C.P.*

[1] NLW MSS Schedule Cilgwyn Estate Papers Group 3. Introduction.
[2] Jones, F. (2000).
[3] Edward A. L. Fitzwilliam pers. comm.
[4] Mitchell, A., *A Field Guide to Trees of Britain and northern Europe.* Collins Europe (1974).

Coedmore, Coedmor

LLANGOEDMOR

Just upstream from Cardigan the Teifi changes abruptly from estuary to gorge, describing a wide U-shape before reaching Llechryd with its second bridgeable point from the sea. Coedmore sits on the wooded south-western edge of a plateau 100ft above the water where it reaches its tidal limit, two miles above Cardigan. Late 18th-century travellers with the picturesque in mind considered the dramatic view south towards Cilgerran Castle to be one of its most praiseworthy features. One wrote in 1798 that 'The two remaining round towers of this fortress, with its ivied walls, present a noble object from the opposite groves of COIDMORE.' Another in 1793 thought that 'In the hands of a man of taste and fortune Coidmore might be rendered one of the most beautiful spots in Europe.'[1] This was potentially to happen in the next generation.

A site such as this will have been occupied since earliest times. Horsfall-Turner quotes Edward Lhuyd's notes of two megalithic monuments, Llech yr Ast and Llech y Gawres (stones respectively of bitch and giantess), in this area.[2] In the Middle Ages the site was noteworthy as a seat of the Mortimer family, who lived somewhere hereabouts at a place known as Castell Cevil, Cefil or Kefael. The property of Coedmore came to the Lewes family of Abernantbychan/Llysnewydd and then the Lloyds of Cilgwyn in the 17th century.

In 1602 George Owen of Henllys recorded the 'big wood' (*coed mawr*) that gave Coedmore its name as being one of the largest in Cardiganshire, and over the river it must have fused with contiguous Cilgerran Forest. Its subsequent depletion was partly the result of industries encouraged by the owners of Coedmore, including the tinworks of

Coedmore Forge at Llechryd in the early 1700s and slate quarrying at Cilgerran in the 1800s: the image of workmen transporting slates by lighter to Cardigan and then exporting them via locally built (wooden) ships illuminates lower Tivyside's erstwhile role as trade corridor and moneymaker for the estates on its banks. One legacy today is a nature reserve conserving the remnants of ancient native woodland.

The garden history of Coedmore presents two possible phases. We should mark the date 1694 and return to it later. There is no doubt that the layout visible today is the result of an early 19th-century renovation of perhaps a

The old house at Coedmore viewed from Cilgerran Castle. Engraving c. 1800.　　*Private Collection*

slightly earlier house. A view of Coedmore *c.*1810 shows a compact three-bay house with its façade facing the river, and two distant cottages marking the sites of the home farm and the walled gardens. Vast improvements took place in the following years. Nicholson in 1813 saw nothing remarkable, but by 1830 the 1-inch OS map showed new approach drives to the north-facing entrance of an irregularly shaped building and in his 1833 edition Lewis acclaimed the house as 'a noble mansion'.

The refurbished Coedmore belongs to the era of Thomas Lloyd (1793–1857), a celebrated athlete who might serve as a good example of *mens sana in corpore sano*. His public career embraced JP, Deputy Lieutenant, High Sheriff,

Lord Lieutenant and Custos Rotulorum. He also showed remarkable prowess in less respectable fields. H.M. Vaughan[3] gleefully recounts how Lloyd shocked an assize judge by pointing out that the coachman who was driving them and the footman in attendance were two of his illegitimate progeny. (He provided accommodation on his estates for his mistresses and employment for their offspring.) There were also four sons from his marriage to Charlotte Longcroft, and further generations of Lloyds ensured the presence of a Lloyd at Coedmore until the 1960s.[4]

The new house dates to some time after his maturity: he inherited the property in 1810 on the death of his father, the Thomas Lloyd who had inherited only one-third of the Cilgwyn estate (see page 24), but who compensated by purchasing the farm of Forest, a stone's throw north-west across the valley from Coedmore, in Pembrokeshire. Perhaps his marriage in 1819 to Miss Longcroft, who was to inherit half of the substantial Llanina estates from her godfather Edward Warren Jones, JP, on his death in 1829, was an inspiration or an incitement.

In the early 19th century the immediate surroundings of the house were laid out as lawn, contained by terracing, revetment walls or ha-ha according to the lie of the land, and laced with various paths and garden buildings, plus specimen trees. This arrangement has prevailed with minor variations till today. Far more interesting are the broader pleasure grounds infiltrating the indigenous woodland downriver and to the north-west of the house, now accessible to the public as Coedmor National Nature Reserve, notable for small-leaved lime, ash, wych elm and wild service tree amidst predominant oak. Here several streams draining the plateau converge to form a valley of sufficiently negotiable gradient to allow a functional (and doubtless ancient) track to descend to an extensive water meadow and

Coedmore seen today across the Teifi from Cilgerran Castle.

river level. Near the bottom, above flood level, are traces of Ferry Cottage, its 19th-century role as shelter for leisure-seeking boating and fishing parties marked by overgrown box and laurel. The early 19th-century landscapers enhanced the woodland with a network of paths, steps and bridges still traceable today, and with exotic trees including beech and conifers. These 19th-century woodland walks are characterized by an edging of large irregular slate slabs set face-on, their interstices patched with vertical infill.

An odd, roughly oval, rubble-walled enclosure occupies a high bluff to the south of the river track, perhaps 150m from the house. A spreading yew tree, a row of beech planted along parts of the wall and the ruins of a 'gazebo', puzzlingly looking inland rather than out over the Teifi, identify this as a planned garden feature, the object of a relatively short but strenuous walk from the house. The 1890 OS map shows a pattern of paths within the enclosure, but the *Register*'s suggestion that this originated as some cruder, earlier feature seems plausible.

Another well-planned walk punctuated by lime trees leads along the margin of the plateau

An early 19th-century watercolour of Ferry Cottage with Coedmore Mansion in the background.

northwards to the walled garden complex, some 500m from the main house as the crow flies but a great deal further on the ground. Gateways built with dressed stone suggest the routes by which the gentry were expected to enter the gardens. The layout here is complicated by the moderately sloping terrain, and instead of a single rectangular enclosure the garden consists effectively of a series of three long rectilinear terraces designed to maximize sun and shelter, with stone walls serving partly as retaining walls. Areas of brick mark the location of glasshouses, most of them lost or ruinous. The evolution of the kitchen garden would have reflected the prestigious status of a house like Coedmore, and it might be possible to trace the succession of garden structures, glasshouses, frames and heating technology. Much of this reconstruction has to be speculative. Here it may be worth recalling H.M. Vaughan's theory regarding Coedmore: 'The present house is of comparatively modern erection, for the old mansion stood nearly a mile to westward; however, the fine walled gardens remain on their original site. They contain a picturesque gazebo with a steep roof, which bears the date "1694"…'. The gazebo is no longer there, but Vaughan's idea may contain a germ of truth. It became an 18th-century convention to build kitchen gardens at a considerable distance from the house, but it is possible that at Coedmore it was the house that was relocated to a more fashionably picturesque spot with a dramatic view.

Coedmore house and its service courtyard are now divided into several separate dwellings, and the home farm and garden house are also privately owned.   *P.D.*

The gazebo, improbably dated 1694, that used to stand in the walled gardens. Early 20th-century photograph.

[1] Henry Skrine quoted in Mavor vol 4 p. 190; and M.W. Thompson (ed.), *The Journeys of Sir Richard Colt Hoare through Wales and England 1793-1810* (1983) pp. 40-42.
[2] Vaughan, H.M., *South Wales Squires* (1926) pp. 99–100.
[3] Jones, Francis, 'Lloyd of Gilfachwen, Cilgwyn and Coedmore', in *Ceredigion* VIII, 1 (1976) pp. 72–99.

Cwmcoedwig, Cwmedwig
LLANYCHAEARN

This tall somewhat stark Victorian mansion stands in a commanding position overlooking the Ystwyth valley just outside Llanfarian. Drainpipe heads attest that it was built in 1870 on the site of Cwmedwig, which was a part of the property owned by James Davies of Ffosrhydgaled. There seems to have been a tradition of using Cwmedwig as a dower house, for in 1841 it had been home to James's widowed mother.

James's son Morris was to inherit Ffosrhydgaled, while Cwmcoedwig would accommodate Morris's five older unmarried sisters and, on her widowhood, their mother. Its tall proportions, and the striking use of courses of yellow brick amongst the grey local gritstone, give it a lively appearance picked out in undulating yellow lines. Nicholas in 1872 described it as 'an elegant residence in the mixed gothic style which has command of still more charming scenery.'

Some parts of the farm buildings which adjoin it to the north, especially the gable end with pigeon loft, may derive from the earlier Cwmedwig farm shown on the tithe map, but the landscaping of the grounds was consistent with the privacy which a ladies' residence might expect. The ground between the mansion and the road descends to a terraced lawn supported on a high retaining wall which effectively concealed the house from the eyes of passers by without impeding the spectacular views across the valley.

The handsome gateway to the south-east with wrought-iron carriage gates and an adjoining pedestrian gate led a carriage drive to the house. Ornamental plantings flanking the drive included golden Irish yew, hiba *Thujopsis*

Cwmcoedwig from the west.

dolabrata, Chamaecyparis pisifera 'Squarrosa' and calico bush *Kalmia latifolia*. Within the lawn were specimens Douglas fir *Pseudotsuga menziesii*, deodar *Cedrus deodara*, silver fir *Abies alba*, oak, beech and sycamore. The roadside margin was screened with *Rhododendron ponticum* and contained behind a six-strand wire and post fence upon which stretching cogs ensured the wire tension. Behind the house was a walled garden containing a greenhouse on the south-facing wall, orchard trees, and the usual marginal and cross paths. This was built contemporaneously with the house and demolished in 1996. Between the house and the former walled garden there survive screening trees, three holm oaks *Quercus ilex*, Scots pines *Pinus sylvestris*, Austrian pine *P. nigra* and a beech.

Three of the sisters remained spinsters, involving themselves in parish activities and in competitive singing by the Llanychaearn choir. One sister, Elizabeth Jane, married Hugh Stephens Richardes of Bryneithin in 1871, and eventually in 1883 at the age of 51 the eldest, Sarah, married T.J. Waddingham of Hafod, aged 43.   *C.P.*

31

Cwmcynfelin
LLANBADARN FAWR

Cwmcynfelin is a mile inland from Clarach bay and is situated part way up the steep, wooded north-facing slope of the valley. It was for many generations the home of the Evans family until it passed from Matthew Evans to his nephew Matthew Davies, a man of considerable influence in Cardiganshire, who married Jane Richardes of Penglais, built the main block of the present house and made large purchases of adjoining land. Their two daughters, the heiresses Anne and Jane, married respectively Isaac Lloyd Williams of Tynywern, and Lewis Davies (later of Tanybwlch), and both continued to reside at their natal home and bring up their nine children, who were born in the first decade of the 19th century.

A handsome estate survey by G. Pugh, 1835-9,[1] enumerates the property of esquires Isaac Lloyd Williams and his eldest son Matthew Davies Williams: the estates of Cwmcynfelin, Tynywern and Cwmrhaidr. The colour plan of the demesne at Cwmcynfelin shows it was approached from Aberystwyth through the rich woodland which clothes the south flank of the Clarach valley, and then via a circuitous private drive which crossed the dingle and avoided the hairpin bend on the public road. A second drive rejoined the road north of the bend. The house looks out north and south across sheltered pleasure grounds planted with specimen trees. The south pleasure ground faces the principal elevation of the house and was laid out with walks and borders, and protected by railings. Beyond these areas were two tastefully laid-out lawns with undulating margins to the enfolding woods and carefully placed clumps of trees. This parkland would have been managed as hay meadow and for grazing, and shows no trace of older field boundaries within it. The 'the lawn above the house' (13 acres) is margined by woodland along the public road, and 'the lawn below the house' (39 acres) extends to the banks of the Clarach river and a screen planting along the far side. The handsome coach house and the home farm, Hengwm, are also carefully screened from view. The woodland east of the pleasure ground is described in the tithe schedule as 'woods – ornamental' and was laced with paths and drives. When the botanist J.H. Salter walked these woods in 1891, he recorded a diverse woodland of beech, horse chestnut, lime, ash, Norway maple, sycamore, mountain ash, whitebeam and birch.[2] Enclosed within it was a small, square, walled garden with cross-paths which was set in the middle of a two–acre hedged kitchen garden containing a gardener's cottage. Shrubbery plants noted by Salter were snowberry and buckthorn. A considerable amount of spurge laurel *Daphne laureola* west of the walled garden was recorded a century later.

N ◄—

The Cwmcynfelin Demesne.
Surveyed by G. Pugh 1835–9.

'Cwm', where Keble composed portions of The Christian Year. Early 20th-century photo.

Opposite the southern gates off the Aberystwyth road, two well-engineered drives explored Cwm Woods west of the road and extended into the adjoining property of Roderick Richardes.

Cwmcynfelin was associated with the Anglican Oxford Movement and John Keble, who often stayed at Cwmcynfelin (and is said to have written part of the hymn collection *The Christian Year* published in 1827 there). Matthew Davies Williams provided the burial ground land and funded £1000 towards the erection of the new Llangorwen church, while his kinsman Roderick Richardes of Penglais provided stone from his quarries. His brother the Revd Isaac Williams preached the sermon in English at the consecration in 1841. The design of the altar and chancel is modelled upon Newman's church at Littlemore. Keble donated the eagle lectern, and sometimes preached there himself.[3]

Matthew Davies Williams died in 1860 and in 1895 the heavily mortgaged estate was bought by Sir Pryse Pryse of Gogerddan.[4] It had several tenants, including David Howells, whose daughter Marjorie became the last chatelaine of Gogerddan.[5] In 1920 it was sold at auction, the catalogue extolling the 'lovely old-world gardens and ornamental grounds, lawns for tennis and croquet, woodland walks, fern walk, flower garden, rose garden and summerhouse.' It then became the home of Principal Davies of the University College of Wales, and was sold again in 1927.[6]

After subsequent changes of use, including a period as a students' hostel during World War II, it has become a residential nursing home. The coach house has been converted to accommodation. The crematorium built in 1994 now looks eastward over what was the 12-acre upper lawn, and the gardener's cottage and walled garden have been replaced by an executive home. However, much of the setting of Cwmcynfelin remains little altered, and on the lawns close to the mansion are some fine specimen trees. The cedar of Lebanon is of similar size to that planted in the early 19th century at Nanteos, while the wellingtonia, also of great size, would have been planted after 1853. There is also a very fine Turkey oak *Quercus cerris* (girth 484cm) and several big English yews, the largest of which had a girth of 378cm in 1992. Cwm Woods, the woodland west of the road, is open to the public and contains footpaths running along the old contoured drive and westward to the old quarry. The woods are rich in beech and sweet chestnut, though very few of these are the original 19th-century trees. When Salter walked here in 1891 he recorded that the woods were mostly fir and larch with some oak and sweet chestnut. The walk affords spectacular views from a dizzy height out over the sheer quarry face towards Clarach and the sea.   *C.P.*

[1] NLW Roberts and Evans Solicitors Records Deposit 1997-8.
[2] NLW Diaries of J.H. Salter 6 November 1891.
[3] Eyre Evans (1903).
[4] NLW MS Cwrt Mawr 1687.
[5] Ceredigion County Archive Box ADX 415 Florrie Hamer papers.
[6] NLW Sale catalogues, Cards. 139, 144.

Derry Ormond

BETWS BLEDRWS

Paradoxically signalled by one of the most conspicuous monuments in the area – the column of Derry Ormond Tower, visible from hilltops for miles around – the fine early 19th-century landscape complex that was one of Ceredigion's prizes began to vanish in the 1950s. Lewis (1833) described 'an elegant modern mansion … beautifully situated under the shelter of a lofty hill covered with luxuriant plantations: the grounds, which are tastefully laid out, are ornamented with a small sheet of water, formed by the expansion of a rivulet by which they are intersected, and over which there is a bridge of handsome design.' Today on the northbound A485, as you enter the village of Betws Bledrws, on your left you still see parkland, a lodge beside a drive and a row of grafted copper beech. But the mansion has gone; the remains of terraced formal gardens lie hidden under shrubbery and the denuded parkland has deteriorated into undistinguished pasture. Some of the bones of the layout are still traceable and include an elaborately conceived picturesque approach to the house involving a splendid series of water features.

Derry Ormond.

Private Collection.

Derry Ormond from an early 20th-century postcard

Of three buildings on the site it is to the grand house designed between 1824 and 1827 by C.R. Cockerell for the third John Jones (1777–1835) that Derry Ormond owes its fame. Early history and the identity of 'Ormond' are obscure. Lhuyd's *Parochialia* recorded that 'Derrywrman is an ancient house in ye parish'. Oak trees felled in the 1950s and uprooted towards the end of the century were reckoned to have been planted 250 years ago by a man called Ormond.[1] The next phase involves more typically 'Cardi' elements. Cattle-dealer and drover David Jones came here in 1741, bought an undescribed house from the Lloyd family of Bronwydd in 1758 and died heavily in debt in 1775. The purchaser was John Jones, a London apothecary and surgeon of local origin, who built a new 'square and compact' house, described by Meyrick in 1810 as 'lately rebuilt and from its elevated situation commanding an extensive view over the surrounding mountains'. His son John II (1745–1817) enlarged the estate considerably by purchasing land cheaply from Thomas Johnes, currently hard pressed to finance his schemes at Hafod (about £17,000 changed hands in ten transactions between 1789 and 1811).[2]

Cockerell was called to Lampeter in 1821 as architect of the newly founded St David's College. John Jones III was involved as treasurer in the project and seized the opportunity to ask Cockerell to design a replacement for his father's house. Cockerell's 'elegant modern mansion' was a two-storey neoclassical villa, seated on massive terracing and embraced by a picturesque parkland setting. Its extensive conservatory echoed that built at Sezincote by Cockerell's father, Samuel Pepys Cockerell, for his brother, Sir Charles, in about 1805. An impression of the design in microcosm can be gained from the later lodge on the A485 (listed grade II), with lunette windows in attic gables.

Modern Derry Ormond's great secret is the remains of the water features north-west of the

The handsome lower bridge over the Dyfel by C. R. Cockerell. Derry Ormond Tower can be seen on the skyline.

road bridge (altered in 2002) along Nant Dyfel, the tributary of the Dulas which Lewis called a rivulet. Just above the bridge was the sawmill, fed by a canalized stretch of stream. Once skilfully camouflaged by shrubbery, this functional watercourse was until recently lost in undergrowth. Further upstream elaborate stonework structures can still be found, although many of these were badly damaged by flooding in the late 20th century.

As Nant Dyfel entered the parkland it was made to widen into a series of three lakes. The top lake was retained by a dam and a stepped spillway to give the sound and visual impression of a waterfall. The middle lake was the largest and had a boathouse. Its dam consisted of a curving vertical wall over which water poured in an impressive cascade. Not far below this, Cockerell's 'handsome' bridge crossed the lowest and smallest of the lakes. This bridge is still standing; today's low water level shows the fine lines of an elegant central arch flanked by large circular overflow holes: when the lake was dammed to its intended level the reflections of these half-concealed openings made it appear triple-arched.

The waterworks and the Reptonian landscaping in the foreground to his fine mansion were Cockerell's own work. In June 1826 he recorded being 'at Derry Ormond marking out lodge, water, bridge etc. Showed Mr Jones approach & drives round the place showing beauties of which he was not before aware.' The main drive was planned to tantalize the arriving visitor in proper picturesque fashion. It forked northwards off the main road (past the terrace of postwar houses now known as Bro Deri), entered the park and made a generous loop to the west before leading north-eastwards up to the house. During the approach visitors would first see the house in the distance, then lose sight of it as they entered a grove of oaks. These and judicious rhododendron planting screened the striking waterscaping which embellished the Dyfel and which would engage visitors' attention from the bridge over the lowest lake, before the house once again came into view. Shrubbery also disguised the difference in water levels, making the two lakes seem one.

Later the drive was diverted westwards and uphill to cross an inferior new 'Victorian' bridge above the lakes. The original bridge became a footbridge which both offered splendid views upstream and formed a picturesque object when viewed from its replacement.

Rerouting the drive changed the experience of visitors approaching the mansion: suspense and surprise were replaced with a more overt display of the sheer extent of the grounds. A new field boundary appeared sometime between 1845 and 1896 (it was removed by 1908). The alteration might have been dictated by agricultural economics in the 1880s, when more intensive grazing of the park was desirable, and was perhaps connected with agreements concerning the letting of the property as a sporting seat in 1865 and 1877.

From 1862 Capt. John Inglis Jones employed William Cotterell (1827–1910) as land agent, a post he retained after Jones's death in 1879. Cotterell must have overseen some of the changes Capt. Jones instituted after coming into his majority in 1850. Some of these were functional, such as building the sawmill to realize some of the estate's timber assets. The house was expanded northwards around 1872, and at some point a balustraded ironwork balcony was added. (It is not visible in the Nicholas engraving.) A comparison of OS maps shows that after 1888 and before 1905 the terracing and formal gardens were substantially extended westwards.

The fortunes of Derry Ormond's owners waxed and then waned. When Wilmot Inglis-Jones (1868–1949) died, the estate was reduced to less than 500 acres (it had reached a peak of 16,000 acres in 1918). Unwanted by the heirs, the mansion was sold for £3,000 and demolished by the new owner in 1952–3: it is said that a profit of £7,000 was made by selling the materials. Modern dwellings have been built near the site of the house and in the walled kitchen garden, where remnants of glasshouses and layout have all but disappeared, and the service buildings have been variously adapted as residences. The core of the site is thus in private ownership. Ornamental shrubbery plantings recorded in 1993 included *Acer negundo*, berberis, deutzias, escallonias, hollies, laburnum and spiraea.

Derry Ormond is like Hafod – an invitation to nostalgia – one of the great 'lost houses' of Ceredigion. Its architectural merits were recognized and it was well documented. Its appearance was from the first recorded in engravings and then in photographs, which help to show successive modifications that can also be traced in maps. More ordinary aspects of garden life were snapped by someone with a camera in the early 1900s, when numbers of photographs were printed as postcards that document gardening personnel and everyday activities as well as conventional scenic views. When the mansion was enlarged in 1872 a photographic dark room was incorporated under the mansard roof.[3] Whether the popular snaps are the result of the owner's personal hobby or whether he inspired other local amateurs remains to be investigated.

Derry Ormond Tower stands on a hill to the south of the park. The grade II★ listed classical column 38.7m tall stands on a square pedestal, its apparent height exaggerated by the narrowing device of entasis. Charles James of Llanddewibrefi is claimed as 'inventor of the Tower at Derry Ormond and the Romantic Arch at Hafod'. Built between 1821 and 1824, it just predates the Cockerell mansion. A gravestone of 1838 in Betws Bledrws churchyard records the tower as 'St David's Pillar'. It is a landmark for miles around. Its effect as an eyecatcher in the mansion's surroundings was ingeniously conceived. Sited just below the brow of the hill, it gave the impression of being within the parkland. Its positioning amounted to more than the aesthetics of 'borrowed landscape': it was an infringement of common rights. The tower was built on common land, for which the estate did not acquire the rights until some 40 years later.   *P.D.*

[1] Inglis-Jones, Elizabeth, 'Derry Ormond', in *Ceredigion*, II, 3 (1954).
[2] Wilks, Austen, 'Derry Ormond Tower: a Welsh landscape artefact' in *Anglo-Welsh Review*, 24 (1975).
[3] Lloyd, Thomas, *Lost Houses of Wales* (1989).

Falcondale

LAMPETER

Falcondale occupies a low bluff overlooking the Nant Creuddyn half a mile north-west of Lampeter. John Battersby Harford (1819–75) could choose from much of the countryside around Lampeter for the site of his new home: the Harford family of Blaise Castle,[1] Bristol, had acquired the extensive Peterwell estates from Richard Hart Davies in 1819. J.B. Harford chose not to rebuild on the Teifiside site of the unfortunate Peterwell, celebrated for its 18th-century rooftop gardens, but to enlarge a modest house across the narrow Creuddyn valley from the Lampeter–Aberaeron turnpike, today's A482.

Cadw in 1992 described the house built in 1859 by Talbot T. Burry of London as in 'Italian villa style on an unusually large scale'. The Italianate influence was perhaps deliberate: in 1850 Harford honeymooned in Italy, which was already familiar to his bride Mary von Bunsen, daughter of the Prussian ambassador to St James's.

An earlier Falcon Dale appears on the 1845 tithe map as a modest house with a service block near by, approached by a single drive that branched in a south-westerly direction from the turnpike. It cannot have been a building of any significance, since the eminent personages who visited Lampeter to discuss with John Scandrett Harford the establishment of St David's College in the early 1820s stayed at Derry Ormond, Highmead, or even Abergwili near Carmarthen, rather than here. 'New and spacious rooms and out-buildings surrounded

the original house of Pant-y-Curyll, anglicized into Falcondale for simplicity's sake,' wrote Alice Harford of the rebuilding. After reading for the Bar, J.B. Harford decided to settle at Falcondale 'and gradually to bring order out of the chaos into which the estate had sunk, and to provide decent houses and buildings for the tenants.' J.B. Harford's motivation contained a hint of the Harford family's Quaker philanthropy. 'If Falcondale were like Blaise Castle and Lampeter like Henbury, I might sit down quietly to enjoy the annual accession to

Private Collection.

'Falcondale from a drawing, 1870', inscribed 'Talbot Bury Architect'.

my capital … but this is … out of the question as long as cottages remain to be built and schools to be encouraged.' Much of Lampeter's character is due to the improving ideas of the Harford family.

Landscaping the surroundings of Falcondale was also a priority. Leisurely drives were flung out to provide access from north and south, hedges visible on the tithe map were removed and copses and shelter belts planted. The course of the Creuddyn was adjusted and a water garden laid out in Pond Wood. (Paths, bridges and islands shown on the 1888/1904 OS map survived and remained accessible into the 1950s.) The turnpike was suitably screened with trees and provided an opportunity for building two lodges, a modest cottage 'in simplified Gothic style' marking the old drive, and the small but showy North Lodge whose Italianate style echoes that of Falcondale. Another Italianate design (Pontfaen Lodge) at the original southern approach from Lampeter is now modified beyond recognition. Later the model Home Farm, Maestir School (now in the Museum of Welsh Life), Maestir Church and paired estate workers' cottages, often hidden in woodland, were added to Harford's growing list of 'decent buildings'.

Around the enlarged house well-planted pleasure grounds ornamented with quartzite rockwork contained a shell house and an encaustic-tiled shelter. Functional items included an ice house and a kitchen garden with brick-lined walls and glasshouses, backed by a generous frame yard. (The ice house is still intact, but the inner walls and backsheds of the neglected walled garden were bulldozed in September 2002.)

The Harford family enjoyed Falcondale for just under a century. The estate was sold, largely to tenants, in the early 1950s and the

The Harford children and companions in September 1904 at 'the pond tea-party' in Pond Wood, the water garden laid out beside the Creuddyn that is now overgrown.

woodland timber was reaped for short-term profit. The mansion became an old people's home for 20 years before being turned into a hotel. Today the pleasure grounds have shrunk to smooth lawns and smart flower beds in the immediate vicinity of the house. A fine copper beech marks the start of the pleasure grounds at the end of the main drive leading from Lampeter. Surviving Victorian conifers include a handful of varieties of *Chamaecyparis lawsoniana* in varying states of health, and Falcondale is one of only three gardens in the county to contain an incense cedar *Calocedrus decurrens* (girth 317cm). Handsome fastigiate yews punctuate the lawn to the east of the house, near the tennis court, and a fine spreading bush of golden yew 15m in diameter graces the lawn in front of the mansion. Birch, fothergilla, witch hazel and cornus are among the garden's subtler plantings. A phalanx of colourful old rhododendron cultivars helps to form a charming backdrop for wedding photographs.   *P.D.*

Mollie Harford and a friend rowing on Falcondale Lake (then known as Henfeddau Lake), some half-mile north-east of the mansion. Photograph c. 1907.

[1] J.S. Harford employed John Nash and George Repton to design Blaise Hamlet, completed 1811.
Also see:
Harford, Alice, *Annals of the Harford Family* (1909).
David, Penny, 'Falcondale: a Victorian Vision', in WHGT *Bulletin*, winter 1994.

Ffosrhydgaled, Conrah

LLANYCHAEARN

The Conrah Country House Hotel overlooks the small community of Chancery, which nestles in a sharp dip in the main Aberystwyth to Aberaeron road. It trades under an eccentric name bestowed upon it by its purchasers in 1967, **Con**stance and **R**onald **A**lfred **H**ughes, manufacturers of pressed metal knick-knacks, who named their hotel and restaurant venture after their joint acronym. Previously to this, it was the home of the Davieses of Ffosrhydgaled.

This family of Davies first came to Ffosrhydgaled from Cardigan in 1753. By 1829 a descendant, Morris Davies, was a substantial figure in Aberystwyth, High Sheriff, corn merchant and owner of the several Trefechan lime kilns. After his death, his nephew James Davies inherited in 1835, and also served as High Sheriff, Deputy Lieutenant and JP. The tithe survey of 1845 shows a quadrangular farmstead and a separate house placed slightly to the east of it, facing out north-east over a large sloping field towards the hamlet of Chancery.

The present house occupies the same site and aspect but was much enlarged. It was described by Nicholas in 1872 as 'in domestic style of architecture and erection, and standing on a slope commanding a view of the beautiful Vale of Ystwyth.' By 1876 James's son Morris Davies (barrister and owner of 749 acres yielding £716 annually)[1] had inherited

Ffosrhydgaled, and his mother and sisters were installed at nearby Cwmcoedwig.

The grounds, as depicted in the OS survey of 1888, show a generous new drive approaching the front of the house. Behind it, and screened by trees, are utilitarian buildings: parts of the old farm, stables, outhouses and a water mill, which are approached by the older, more southerly entrance from the turnpike. There has also been much planting of trees to form a sheltering belt of mixed plantation to the west, south and east of the mansion, and

'Ffosrhydgaled after the disastrous fire of April 1911'. Arthur Lewis Photo Album 711.

extending to impark the margins of the field below the house. West of the house is a kitchen garden with a single freestanding greenhouse. The setting of the house was protected by a stone ha-ha. It overlooked grazing animals in the ovoid field, parkland lime trees and the view of the picturesque Chancery cottages and school (built 1870).

In 1911 the entire building was spectacularly gutted by fire. The house was rebuilt on the same site, and much of the garden layout remained unaltered. However, much rubble from the fire damage was used to extend the ha-ha in a north-westerly direction such that it now creates a lawned causeway past the kitchen garden. The ha-ha, and a pedestrian stepway into the park, were capped in curved blue engineering brick. A summerhouse and tennis court were built on the grassed level terrace east of the house.

The plantations around the house and at the east margin of the park are principally beech and a few Douglas firs *Pseudotsuga menziesii*. Tree-ring counts of windblown beeches in 1990 showed them to be have been seedlings in the 1860s. Three substantial limes *Tilia vulgaris* remain, two in the park, and one at the north-east corner of the house. To the west of the house is a small pinetum containing Douglas fir, *Cryptomeria japonica* 'Elegans', *Thujopsis dolabrata, Thuja plicata*, Irish yew, Scots pine *Pinus sylvestris* and Austrian pine *P. nigra*. The shrubbery east of the house is planted with popular evergreens: *Rhododendron ponticum*, cherry laurel, Portugal laurel, Highclere holly, variegated holly and fastigiate yews. An extensive system of rills drains the shrubbery and is bridged by slate or concrete slabs.

The kitchen garden, which was never walled, but hedged with cherry laurel and privet, was substantially altered after 1904 to create a more informal approach from the house. It is managed as a productive flower and vegetable garden for the hotel. An exit through a hedge of *Lonicera nitida* in the north-west margin leads to a further evergreen shrubbery in native woodland to the west of the park. Near by are a number of cherry plums *Prunus cerasifera*, locally common at the site of old gardens, and exceptional in regularly producing fruit.

There is a persistent history that the mansion was bought by the Smiths Crisps family in 1929. In fact, the wealthy Misses Smith who bought Ffosrhydgaled were from Glasgow, and their fortune derived from tar macadam. Discovering the house whilst holidaying in Wales, they settled here and bought the first Rolls Royce in the area. Their chauffeur, Roberts, went on to found the local bus company of that name.   *C.P.*

[1] Owners of Land, Wales (1875).

Ffosrhydgaled: the ha-ha east of the mansion.

CDP 1996

Glandyfi Castle, Dovey Castle

LLANFIHANGEL GENAU'R-GLYN,
YSGUBOR Y COED

Six miles south of Machynlleth, and just within the county of Ceredigion, the road and the railway are squeezed close between rising ground and the river Dyfi where it broadens into salt-flats and marshes. Perched above, atop a nearly sheer slope, and commanding a spectacular panorama north-westerly across the estuary, is an exquisitely designed Regency gothick castle, with mullioned windows, square, round and octagonal towers, and irregularly placed chimneys, some square, and some round. This house and its mature pleasure grounds were laid out in the early 19th century by an unknown architect for George Jeffreys and his wife Justina.[1] To the south of it are a number of houses and gardens whose history is linked to that of the castle; these are now known as Ranger Lodge, Voelas, The Mill House and Llwyncelyn.

In the 17th century this area of land was called Garreg, and had a very different appearance. This had been poor farmland and woodland until its mineral wealth was discovered, and the smelting houses and refining mills of the Royal Mines Adventurers of England invaded the landscape. By the beginning of the 18th century some north

Ceredigion landowners, such as the Pryses of Gogerddan, were making a fortune from silver and lead. It was probably for this reason that Edward Jeffreys of Shrewsbury (1715-1801) was eager to become an investor in the area. In 1768 he invested £1000 in purchasing a half-share in Shrewsbury businessman Henry Bowdler's mining leases on lands belonging to Gogerddan and Ynyshir estates. The jewel in this portfolio of mines, rakes, beds, holes, and

A Seat, 5 miles from Machynlleth, in Montgomeryshire.

Sketch from A Tour of Scenery in Wales by John Masleni, 1826.   *NLW*

veins of lead, tin and copper ore was the smelting works at Garreg with its furnaces, refining slag-hearth, and machinery.[2]

Jeffreys owned some land at Garreg which adjoined an existing mill on the Melindwr stream belonging to Mr Skryme of Pembrokeshire. In 1787 he leased 2 acres of it to the Machynlleth merchant Francis Chalmers who was to invest a considerable amount of money in developing a new corn mill or manufactory upon it. In 1792 Jeffreys took the

Glandovey Castle. Early 20th-century postcard.

opportunity to purchase most of the village of Eglwysfach and the farms of Ynysfach and Blaencletwr, Tre'r-ddôl, from the widow Mrs Skryme of Pembrokeshire.[3] Having thus acquired the old Garreg mill adjoining his land, he agreed a new 60-year lease with Chalmers of 'a newly erected building intended to be made into a mill or manufactory, a dwelling house, a counting house and office adjoining thereto, a drying kiln, and dwelling-house opposite thereto, and the mill pool, weir and waterstream' on condition that the mill be completed within two years, and that Jeffreys retained the timber and mineral rights.[4] Edward Jeffreys died aged 86 in 1801, and his memorial stands in St Edmund's Church, Shrewsbury. Garreg, for him, had been an industrial speculation, not a home.

The impetus to build Glandyfi Castle arose as a result of the untimely death of Edward Jeffrey's eldest grandson, while serving in the Peninsular War in 1812. The estate passed to his brother George. Here were combined all the ingredients for visionary extravagance and ostentatious home-building. Aged just 23 when he inherited, George was a burgess of Shrewsbury and had been admitted as an attorney to the King's Bench in 1811.[5] In 1814 he married Justina Scott of Penhelig, Aberdovey, a young woman who, it has been claimed, was the model for the accomplished but unconventional Anthelia in Thomas Love Peacock's novel *Melincourt*. Justina was already a friend of the aspiring author, who attributed her literary and poetic sensibilities to the influence of her scholarly uncle Edward Scott of Bodtalog, Tywyn. She had been born Justina McMurdo in Jamaica in 1788 and it is suggested that she was adopted by her 'uncle' and his new wife, the widow Louisa Maria de Saumaise, who, through her father Lewis Anwyl, had inherited Bodtalog. Certainly an attachment is indicated by the fact that Justina and George's first daughter was named Louisa

The late 19th-century lawned terraces behind the castle.

Maria. Throughout his long life, Edward Scott cultivated many literary friends, Welsh and English.[6]

To Justina and George, a Picturesque castle on the Dyfi would have spelt the height of fashion and taste, and the choice of location exploited the added historical romance associated with castles of antiquity. In the 11th century Machynlleth was protected by a Welsh earth-and-timber castle on a promontory on the river below, and this structure had been succeeded by a 12th-century stone castle constructed in the vicinity by Roger de Clare. Equally important, the recently constructed turnpike taking its route along the banks of the Dyfi rendered the hill at Garreg romantically remote, yet also an accessible and plainly visible location, just out of sight of the mill and adjoining functional buildings,

The Jeffreys estate also included land and property in Chester, Montgomeryshire and Shropshire, but George and Justina settled immediately at Glandyfi and probably lived in the house now known as Ranger Lodge while their castle was being built. When their first two daughters were christened at Eglwysfach church in 1815 and 1816, the Jeffreys' abode was recorded as 'Glandovey', but by the birth of the first son in 1818, Dovey Castle was complete. A further six children were born there in the following ten years. Like his wife's family, Jeffreys seems to have been something of an aesthete; he possessed a library which he deemed sufficiently important to designate as an heirloom in his will. When Thomas Love Peacock married Jane Gruffydd in 1820 the bride took temporary residence in the Chapelry of Eglwysfach at Glandyfi Castle, and George Jeffreys and the Revd George Scott of Penhelig, Aberdovey, were the witnesses. Peacock visited the Jeffreys family on other occasions in the following decade.

A letter from Aneurin Owen to his father William Owen Pughe in 1824 describes an expedition: 'Mr Jeffreys of Glandyfi Castle came over here one day and took me with him to see his house. It is built in the castellated style, is a pretty object on the banks of the river and the prospect is delightful.'[7] Thomas John Masleni, travelling and sketching in autumn 1826 also gave an enthusiastic account, but clearly knew nothing of the occupants. 'At the 12th milestone passed a small but truly well imitated gothic castle on the top of a small hill, backed by high hills and looking down on the valley, the beautiful windings of the river and the bay....several very large sloops in the river and one having a new keel made for it. A fine pleasure boat at the foot of

Ranger Lodge, formerly Glandŵr. Early 20th-century postcard.

the castle hill. While taking a sketch of the castle a fashionable Party of Male and Female equestrians and a car[8] with two handsome girls passed me. Lost sight of the seat at 14 miles'.[9] The river was navigable to a quay at Garreg for vessels of up to 300 tons burden and carried a lively trade.[10]

The tithe survey of 1845 shows the castle set in 21 acres of established gardens, plantations and shrubberies. It was approached through castellated gateposts, past a modest lodge cottage, and up an inclined hairpin drive which left the turnpike north of the track leading to the mill and manufactory. The wooded pleasure grounds are contemporaneous with the house. Substantial two-hundred-year-old trees include a fine grove of beeches north-east of the castle, several of which have been bunch-planted, two or more saplings to a single hole, such that in growth they fuse together to form massive multi-trunked trees. Huge silver firs *Abies alba* date from the early plantings, as may a sweet chestnut *Castanea sativa* near to the long rectangular walled garden which follows the strike of the slope south of the ornamental areas. This was a utilitarian kitchen garden, not built for greenhouses and exotics, or lined with brick. It had a small bothy at ´ the bottom corner and a path running down the long axis, linking neat arches of splayed rubble stone in the end walls. Footpaths through the pleasure grounds linked the castle to cottages on the roadside to north and south. The two cannons which still ornament the castle are said to have been used in the Crimean war, and were given to George Jeffreys by Robert Davies Pryce of Cyfronnydd in Montgomeryshire.[11]

The tithe map also shows Glandovey Cottage (later known as Glandŵr, and then as Ranger Lodge) to be a gentleman's house, set about with garden and shrubbery and mature trees. It was by now the home of George's eldest son Edward Jeffreys and his wife. The mill and premises continued as a working, tenanted concern, and, along with two tenant farms, Melindwr and Ynysfach, accounted for a total holding of 487 acres of income-generating land in the parish. When George Jeffreys died aged 78 in 1868, his wife Justina survived him for less than two years, and the estate passed to his eldest son Edward, while his unmarried daughters Georgiana and Jessie resided, on substantial annuities, in Glandovey Cottage (now Glandŵr Lodge) and Rhos (later Rose) Cottage. On Edward's death in 1888 the estate and its debts passed to the third son, Charles, who returned from his farm in New Zealand[12] and occupied it with his wife and daughter from 1891[13] until his death in 1904.

During the second half of the 19th century, a greater diversity of exotic trees was introduced to the pleasure grounds. These include a monkey puzzle, a wellingtonia, and numerous cultivars of the Lawson cypress. Close to the lower drive is a very fine Lucombe oak *Quercus* x *crenata*, and in the lawn north-east of the castle is a mulberry *Morus nigra*. The lawned area south-east of the house was levelled into a series of terraces, rising to a croquet lawn and tennis courts beyond. Also a fine variety of large-flowering hybrid rhododendrons was introduced to the gardens. By the end of the century the industrial past of Francis Chalmers's Garreg was just a memory, the corn mill had fallen into disuse and the millpond was empty. One of these buildings had, by 1870, become another 'gentleman's residence' leased out by the Jeffreys family, and was known as Dovey Bank. In the sale catalogue of 1906 it is described as substantially improved, with well-stocked fruit and kitchen gardens and a flower garden overlooking the waterfall.[14]

The estate was divided at auction in 1906, and the castle and 370 acres was bought by Lewis Pugh Evans Pugh (recently of Abermâd), who immediately sold on the castle and 43 acres to Major Robert John Spurrell, while retaining the rest of the land. Pugh's granddaughter, Mrs Joy Neal, now occupies Llwyncelyn. Glandyfi Castle and its pleasure grounds had a series of owners, including, in the 1950s, the BSA motorcycle company owned by Sir Bernard Docker. Accused, in a shareholder rebellion, of profligate refurbishment with company money – 'Extravagance? What about that castle in Wales?…furnished for £30,000, like the Ritz' – BSA hastily disposed of the castle.[15] It appears that few alterations were made to the grounds in the 20th century, except for the lilypond and fountain on the site of the former croquet lawn, which were installed by Bettina and Harry Lancaster, who bought the castle in 1962. The garden is well maintained and has great charm. To the south of it, Dovey Bank was further aggrandized and landscaped and became renowned for its summer bedding. Its name was changed to Voelas. Two formerly modest buildings now boast very fine gardens which can be visited through the National Gardens Scheme. One is The Mill House, its pool once more filled with water, and the other is Llwyncelyn (a house built upon a plot sold in the 1906 auction) whose gardens incorporate the Dovey Bank kitchen garden, an extensive woodland garden and a new arboretum. Glandyfi Castle is not open to the public. *C.P.*

[1] NLW B.R.A. 1963 Welsh deeds 1110 &1026/23.
[2] NLW deeds 829.
[3] Meyrick, and deed of 1 May 1792
[4] NLW, B.R.A. 1963, Welsh deeds, 1110 & 1026/16a, 16b
[5] NLW, B.R.A. 1963, Welsh deeds 1110 & 1026/19
[6] Madden, M. & Madden, L., 'Edward Scott, Bodtalog, and his literary circle', in *NLW Journal* 24, pp. 352–7 (1986).
[7] NLW MS 136263C. letter from Aneurin Owen 23 July 1824.
[8] From the 16th century, 'car' was a poetic or grandiose term for a wheeled vehicle. *OED.*
[9] NLW Additional MS 65A p.91.
[10] Lewis (1833).
[11] NLW MS Will of George Jeffreys.
[12] http://library.christchurch.org.nz/Heritage/LocalHistory/Fendalton/FendaltonMemories.asp
[13] Census 1891.
[14] NLW Sale Catalogue Cards. 62.
[15] *Daily Telegraph* 18 July 1956.

Gogerddan
LLANBADARN FAWR

Gogerddan mansion nestles between two wooded hills west of Penrhyn-coch, close to the confluence of several tributaries of the Clarach, where the land opens out into a broad flood plain reaching to the sea at Clarach bay. This is one of the four big Cardiganshire estates, home of the Prys ap Rhys family whose squires wielded great influence. Richard Pryse served as MP for Cardiganshire for many terms between 1584 and 1622 and was knighted in 1603. During the 17th century lead and silver were being extracted on Gogerddan lands under leases granted by the Crown, and these activities were vigorously opposed by his grandson, also Richard Pryse (who none the less acquired a baronetcy in 1641). His great-nephew Sir Carbery Pryse, the 4th baronet, enabled further enrichment of this previously agricultural estate by bringing to the statute book the Mines Royal Act of 1693 which allowed landowners to work and profit from their own mines. Following this success, his famous ride from London to Gogerddan has become the stuff of legend. The mansion to which he returned was already by Cardiganshire standards a huge house, assessed in 1672 for hearth tax at 16 hearths.

In the 18th century the baronetcy was extinguished and the estate passed through the hands of a series of Pryse kinsmen who were short-lived and/or childless. In 1765 Gogerddan was home to John Pugh Pryse, aged 25, and his mother Maria Charlotte, who had been widowed for the last 20 years. He, or perhaps his mother, must have been responsible for elaborate plans for the gardens which were drawn by William Coombs in 1765.

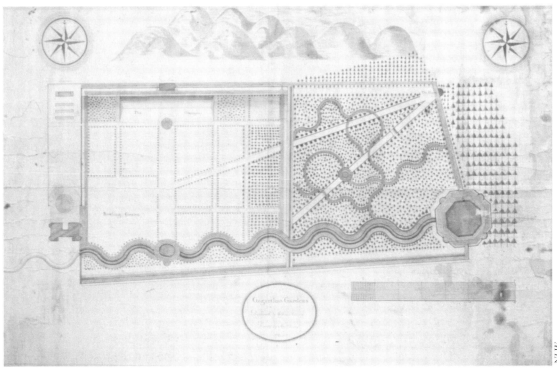

'Gogerthan Gardens.' Designed by William Coombs, drawn by Thomas Lewis, 1765.

In preparation, an accurate survey by Thomas Lewis showed the layout of the existing gardens and the precise footprint of the mansion and associated buildings in 1765.[1] The ornamental garden lay to the east of the mansion, and consisted of a tapering quadrangle of eleven plats and two orchards. The north and west margins of the garden appear to have been bounded by walls and the path along the north margin was furnished with a recessed alcove. To the east, an avenue of trees extended from the formal garden, while to the south the garden was bounded by the course of the Nant Silo. A mill leat ran parallel with the natural streambed, serving a mill pond and mill, before rejoining the main stream west of the mansion.

Coombs's elaborate plan would have been very costly and may have taken insufficient account of the lie of the land. His rectangular walled garden east of the mansion was divided into formal plats and centred upon a square bowling green. Further east was a two-part wooded pleasure ground cut by convergent *allées* and laced with circuitous paths. The Nant Silo was to be canalized in a regularly undulating course running from an octagonal to an oval pool and then margining three sides of the bowling green before continuing in front of the house. To the north there was to be a large orangery and smaller greenhouse inside the walls, and a row of four square gardens quartered by paths outside it. The rising ground beyond was to be a plantation cut by convergent *allées* leading to a focal point at the top.[2]

A second plan, 'Gogerthan Gardens designed by William Coombs, drawn by Thomas Lewis 1765', includes many of these elements in a somewhat more modest form.[3] Here the Silo does not form a canal around the bowling green, which is approached directly from the house. The garden is walled only on its west and north extremities and the pleasure

ground is somewhat simplified. It is none the less an ostentatious design, well furnished with hothouses, greenhouse and a very large orangery. John Pugh Pryse, who had served as MP for Cardiganshire and for Merionethshire, died unmarried aged 34 in 1774, and his grieving mother erected an exceptionally fulsome memorial in Llanbadarn Church recording his 'lively genius' and other qualities. The garden design seems never to have been implemented, but the triangular form of the plantation to the north may date from this time. Coombs was later retained as road surveyor by the Turnpike Trustees (1770-88).

Gogerddan passed briefly to Lewis Pryse and thus to his daughter Margaret, wife of Edward Loveden Loveden of Buscot Park, Berkshire. The old formal garden was swept away and replaced by parkland, which appears newly planted in an oil painting showing the east front.[4] To the south of the road to Penrhyn-coch an unspectacular one-acre produce garden, walled on three sides, was laid out on 26 October 1780 in Cae Tan-y-Coed Issa. Subsequent to Margaret Pryse's death in 1784 an estate plan of Gogerddan lands was drawn by Richard Davies of Lewknor, Oxon, in 1787.[5] Her husband and son dwelt at Buscot and only the mansion, the walled kitchen garden and 114 acres of plantation and woodland north and south of the mansion remained 'in hand'. The parkland fields, 'the green' and 'the lawn' adjoining the mansion were occupied as pasture by the tenant William Poole of Peithyll farm. The north margins of the parkland had by now been softened by scalloped plantations of trees on the margin of the plantation.

A second estate survey was drawn by Richard Morgan in 1836 for Margaret's son, Pryse Pryse.[6] The walled garden remains to the south of the road and the narrow strip of land between Nant Silo and the road is planted as an informal pleasure ground. North of the

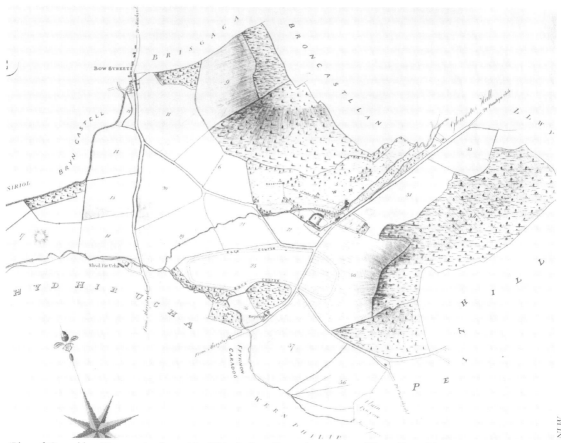

'Plan of Gogerddan Demesne in the parish of Llanbadarn Fawr, the property of Pryse Pryse Esq., by Richard Morgan land surveyor, 1836.'

mansion, the lawn and the green have been amalgamated to form a parkland with further clusters of specimen trees, and a new approach drive has been created from the north-west which brought carriages to a turning circle at the north side of the house. Thomas Roscoe rode past the south side of Gogerddan, on the public road to Penrhyn-coch in 1836. 'Shortly, in a narrow but avenue-like lane you pass Gogerddan, the mansion of Mr Pryse, surrounded by all of comfort, luxury and beauty that nature and art may combine for man's enjoyment.'[7] Pryse Pryse was no gardener, but his sporting enthusiasms are reflected by the racecourse occupying the flat land west of the demesne and by the kennel

enclosure attached to the south end of the walled garden. The oval racecourse was bisected by the road from Aberystwyth to Penrhyn-coch; its site is now crossed by the A4159 to Bow Street.

By the time of the 1887 OS survey the kennels had gone and the kitchen garden had been extended south-east to almost double its capacity. It contained eleven glassed greenhouses or frames. A walled orchard adjoined the gardens. A large part of the mansion had been rebuilt and a designed lodge with gothic windows had been erected where the new drive leaves the public road. The scalloped plantings on the edge of the plantation (now known as Fir Wood) were the

A View of Plas Gogerddan, oil, c 1784. The ten-year-old Pryse Loveden (later Pryse Pryse) is seen frolicking with his dog. The men in the middle distance appear to be pistol-shooting.

object of a pleasure walk from the mansion and contained a substantial glass summerhouse within an enclosed garden, and a fern gully leading up into the woods beyond. The racecourse was no longer there, and the site contained a pheasantry below Pwll Crwn woods. The then squire, Sir Pryse Pryse, family man, JP and Deputy Lieutenant, was created baronet in 1866. He was a lifelong sportman who died of a foxbite in 1906.

In 1948 the estate was broken up and the *plas* and its lands became the Welsh Plant Breeding Station, now incorporated in the Institute for Grassland and Environmental Research (IGER). Much new building occupies the former site of the walled garden

and the home farm. The old mansion remains, set amongst mature rhododendrons, and there is one very large lime, *Tilia* x *europaea,* west of the house. The entrance lodge is in separate ownership. The park north of the mansion is now subdivided into small fields and an extension of the plantation has engulfed the former scalloped plantings at its margin and the ruins of the summerhouse.   *C.P.*

[1] NLW Maps Gogerddan 117 (RMA 126).
[2] NLW Maps Gogerddan 80.
[3] NLW Maps Gogerddan 115 (RMA 125).
[4] NLW photo PB 03017.tif.
[5] NLW Roll Map C22; NLW Maps Vol 41.
[6] NLW Maps Gogerddan 111.
[7] Roscoe, T. (1837).

Hafod mansion. Steel engraving by Newman and Co., c. 1850.

Hafod

LLANFIHANGEL-Y-CREUDDYN

New visitors to Hafod, the only Cadw/ICOMOS *Register* grade I listed historic landscape in the county, need, perhaps, to be prepared in advance to understand what they will not see. There are no flower gardens at Hafod, no mansion, and few impressive built structures. The landscape is one of nature, modified inconspicuously by the hand of man; it can only be fully enjoyed on foot, and to view the dramatic features of the walks involves considerable distances.

Hafod was the vision of one man, Thomas Johnes, who, with a fortune largely derived from his mother's family, the Knights of Croft Castle in Herefordshire, set about creating his personal Xanadu in the bleak environs of lead mining and sheepwalks of the upper Ystwyth valley twelve miles inland from the sea. These uplands seem very remote even today. In the 18th century they were even more so, though it must be remarked that at that time the route from London to Aberystwyth, such as it was, passed from Rhayader to the Elan valley and Cwmystwyth and thus past the gates of Hafod.[1] Johnes's mansion, set upon a natural platform north of the river, was by Thomas Baldwin and the very picture of modernity in 1788. By 1795 it was further embellished with small pavilions at three corners, and with octagonal library, offices and a long conservatory by John Nash. A snapshot of the glory of its heyday is best afforded by the description by Mavor, who toured through Wales in 1805:

> Hafod is built in a chaste modern gothic style and perfectly assimilates the character of the country in which it is placed. Built of Portland stone, with turrets and painted windows, it is only two storeys high, the valley seems to close at both ends and aptly represents an oasis amidst a surrounding desert. The library itself is one of the most superb octagonal rooms in the kingdom and is filled with many choice and valuable books. From this is a communication with the Conservatory, which is 300 feet long and replete with the most curious plants; but strangers, without special permission are not allowed to examine them.

Below the house, Mavor and his companion 'passed over a lawn where the mowers were at work' (this would be men with scythes, for lawnmowers had yet to be invented) and went towards the trapezoidal kitchen garden on the flood plain by the river. The garden had heated fruit walls and a range of ten glasshouses against them. It 'contained every appendage for furnishing the dessert'.

Mavor turned back at the bridge where the walks commenced, so for the most exhaustive description of what he missed one should turn to George Cumberland's 1796 volume *An Attempt to describe Hafod.*[2] Two circuits, the Lady's and the Gentleman's Walks, were laid out according to the picturesque principles of the late 18th century, both taking advantage of all that was beautiful or sublime, and embellishing nature with diverted and improved cascades, flimsy rustic bridges, passages and caves hewn through the rock, and viewing platforms giving the best perspective on each scene. Along the route were a cold bath for the gentlemen and two further walled gardens, Mrs Johnes's walled flower garden by the drive, and, accessible to the privileged few, his daughter Marianne's private alpine garden, on a bluff high above. In 1805 the monument to agricultural innovator Francis, 5th Duke of Bedford, was erected on the bluff south of Marianne's Garden, and work was nearing completion on the New Walk to the gorge on the Ystwyth upstream of Dologau, and on a chain footbridge across the chasm.

Soon after Mavor wrote his account, Hafod burned in 1807. The family clustered helplessly in their nightclothes watching the inferno. Johnes himself was away in London, and returned to find his library destroyed and home uninhabitable. It was three years before they moved back from temporary accommodation (see Castle Hill) to their lavishly reconstructed home. The next few years, however, were troubled: Marianne, his cherished daughter and heir, died in 1811, his debts mounted and his health deteriorated. On his death in 1816 his widow moved to Devon. The estate was let to tenants, for Johnes's tortuous financial affairs precluded a sale, and the property did not come on the market until 1832 when it was purchased by the Duke of Newcastle.

It would be incorrect to assume that the historic landscape at Hafod, as it is seen today, is entirely a Johnesian legacy, for the Duke of Newcastle and many successive owners made structural additions and alterations.[3] The drive which now runs across the lower lawn below the mansion was the Duke's (built in 1837), while the drive to the mansion from the east, which cuts through a rocky bluff and curves round to reveal the house, was probably built between 1847 and 1855 for Henry de Hoghton. De Hoghton added to the house a vast Italianate wing by Anthony Salvin, which, by more than doubling its size, was eventually to contribute to the unviability of the mansion. Probably he also commissioned designs by W.A. Nesfield for a ha-ha and formal beds east of the house. The present gardener's cottage adjoining the walled garden was built in the mid 19th century and a walled orchard was appended to the kitchen garden. The surviving glasshouses by Messenger & Co are late 19th-century. Hawthorn Cottage, which faces the pond north-east of the mansion, stands upon the footprint of Johnes's Pendre Isaf or

The cascade cavern. Copper engraving after Stothard. Published in Malkin (2nd ed. 1807).

'Menagerie' but was rebuilt in the late 19th century by John Waddingham. The present Lower Lodge at Pontrhydygroes also dates from Waddingham, as does the stable block of 1882. This is now the estate office of the Hafod Trust. In 1941 the then owner, W.G. Tarrant, created the concrete barrage across the river at Dologau, which drove a hydroelectric generator supplying the house, cottages and sawmill.

The cedar of Lebanon on Middle Hill was probably planted in Johnes's time, although others were planted by the Duke. Loudon in 1838 recorded one cedar as 40 years old and 32ft 6in high.[4] Small-leaved limes may have been planted as waymarkers; one *Tilia cordata* marks the start of the footpath up to the Bedford monument and another the return of the Gentleman's Walk to the former 'flying bridge' to the kitchen garden. More exotic trees arrived in the late 19th century, including the wellingtonias on Middle Hill and by the kitchen garden, a cucumber tree *Magnolia acuminata* by the gardener's cottage, Japanese maples behind the mansion, an avenue of conifers along the drive, and a ginkgo, a hiba *Thujopsis dolabrata* and a yellow buckeye *Aesculus flava* in Marianne's garden. All these are probably attributable to the ownership of John Waddingham, followed by his son T.J. Waddingham, which spans the period 1872–1940. The avenue and the ginkgo no longer survive.

During the late 19th century much timber was felled and replanted and the process continued in the 20th century. Little survives of Johnes's extensive planting of oak, beech and larch. In 1958 the now-derelict mansion was dynamited by the Forestry Commission and extensive new conifer planting and forestry tracks imposed insensitively on the former landscape. One track was driven, on a ramp, right through Mrs Johnes's walled garden. The footpaths and estate walks became degraded and overgrown, in places impassable, and were known and loved principally by members of the volunteer pressure group, The Friends of Hafod, which was formed in the 1980s.

It is these paths and the views they visited which have been the focus of the careful restoration by the Welsh Historic Gardens Trust and then the Hafod Trust, in partnership with Forest Enterprise, and supported by the Heritage Lottery Fund and other donors. Visitors now start from the car park adjoining the church, and, if lucky enough to find the church unlocked, may pause to mourn at the elaborate marble sculpture by Sir Francis Chantrey which depicts Thomas and Jane Johnes in attendance as Marianne expires upon a *chaise longue*. This sculpture was never paid for in Johnes's lifetime but was bought by the Duke of Newcastle as an adornment for Hafod church. A conflagration of the church in 1932 has reduced it to shattered fragments.

Following the circuit paths which are now reinstated, for the most part on their original routes, it is easy to identify with the walking culture of Georgian gentry as described in the novels of Jane Austen. High points of the walks today include the Peiran falls, the restored alpine bridge, the walk-through cave, the cascade cavern, and the newly restored chain bridge. Some huge beeches, bunch-planted as saplings to fuse into mighty double- or multiple-trunked trees, survive from Johnes's day, especially on Pant Melyn hill and Allt Dihanog. There are also some venerable oaks and a fine horse chestnut beside the pond at Hawthorn Cottage. A detour from the approach to the alpine bridge takes in the stone beehive-shaped ice house, which is thought to date from Johnes's time, and is the best preserved icehouse in the county.

A guide leaflet is available from a box at the car park or from the Estate Office. Walks are waymarked, but all the houses within the estate are in private occupancy and not open to visitors.   *C.P.*

[1] Ogilby, J., *Britannia Atlas* (1675).
[2] Cumberland, George, *An Attempt to Describe Hafod*, bicentenary edition, ed. Jennifer Macve and Andrew Sclater, Hafod Trust (1996).
[3] Macve, J., 'A History of the Hafod Estate' in *Gerddi*, II, I, pp. 20–32 (1999).
[4] Loudon, J.C., *Arboretum et Fruticetum Britannicum*, IV, p. 1226 (1838).

Also see:
Peacocks in Paradise by Elisabeth Inglis-Jones (1950).
An attempt to Depict Hafod, a collection of annotated illustrations by David S. Yerburgh (2000).

Hafod: the restored chain bridge.

Highmead, Dolau Mawr

LLANWENOG

19

Mature copper beeches lining the A485 Lampeter–Carmarthen road south-west of Llanybydder are the cue to look westwards across the Teifi for glimpses of the romantic-looking Gothic sprawl of Highmead's façade. Closer inspection brings disappointment: motley Victorian 'improvements' have not worn well and both building and setting have the uncared-for air of a place that has too long been an institution. Gardening activity has shrunk to little more than mowing the grass around the mansion and in a sunken rose garden west of the house.

The 'sheltered eminence' of the former Highmead estate looks south over the Teifi just before its leisurely middle course narrows between steep banks. This was a historic site. The legends of the *Mabinogion* tell that the court of Pryderi ap Pwyll was at Rhuddlan, a name that lives on in the area. The 'mead' of Highmead is a translation of the Welsh *dôl*, plural *dolau*. The family is descended from the Lloyds of Castell Hywel, but the garden interest begins when Herbert Evans (1743–87) of Lowmead or Dolau Bach built a new mansion 'near the house of Lowmead (used by his father John Evans as a hunting-lodge) on part of the Llanfechan estate which belonged to his mother.'[1] The 'plain yet commodious' house built in 1776–8 by John Calvert must have been surrounded by suitable gardens: there had already been much tree planting and enclosure.

Highmead's rise to prominence is attributable to Herbert Evans's marriage in about 1769 to Anne, daughter of the Revd Watkin Lewes of Penybenglog, Meline (Pembs.), and sister to Sir Watkin (an intriguing figure, sometime MP and twice Lord Mayor of London, who eventually died a pauper). A wife with a dowry is good news for gardens (Anne's brought her husband property worth some £6000 a year 'but it was so heavily encumbered that he sold it at once'.[2]) Anne must also have brought a great deal of brain. Herbert Evans died in 1787 aged 44, having sired twelve children of which only one eventually had issue. In 1807 a tablet was erected in Llanwenog church to

'Highmead: the Seat of Major Herbert D. Evans' from Nicholas (1872).

commemorate Herbert Evans of Y Dolau Bach and his wife 'Ann Goch'. Herbert's widow, who lived until 1807, managed her household and her dairy herd in a thoroughly businesslike way. Early on his tours through Wales, Richard Fenton drank a glass of wine and ate a biscuit with her in 1804, before proceeding 'though her beautiful plantation to Lampeter.' By 1810, when Meyrick visited the property now belonging to Major Evans, his mother's memory elicited unusual praise: 'It is said of the late Mrs Evans … that though a lady, her agricultural knowledge and practice far exceeds that of any man in the country.³ The scrupulous records she kept of her dairying are a valuable archival source today.⁴ It is likely that horticulture went hand in hand with agriculture in this family of taste.

When he was not engaging in electioneering, Major Evans's contribution to Highmead was arboricultural. Vast quantities of timber were harvested and planted: they say he was awarded a silver medal for tree planting in 1816. A letter of March 1814 from his son-in-law, soon to be Sir George Griffies-Williams of Llwynywormwood (Carms.), makes passing mention of Wellington and Buonaparte but is precise about the trees he is sending by cart to Herbert Evans: 2300 larch, 100 beech, 100 Spanish chestnut, 500 whitethorn ('… the whitethorn I hope you will plant as single trees … I think nothing more ornamental than a hawthorn tree').⁵ Major Evans also created, or expanded, the kitchen garden, which bears an inscribed keystone dated 1820 above the garden door.

In 1817 Major Evans married Elizabeth, widow of W.G. Davies of Penlan and daughter of Lord Robert Seymour of Taliaris (Carms.), but there was no issue. Major Evans was succeeded by his great-nephew. (Major Evans's brother Watkin's daughter had married Capt. Delme Seymour Davies of Penlan (Carms.), and their son Herbert Davies added Evans to his name on succeeding in

Highmead: a game of skittles on the front lawn in 1888. Photo Album 36.

'Natural' planting in the water gardens in the 1880s reflects the ideas of William Robinson. Photo Album 36.

1848.) This Herbert Davies-Evans married a daughter of banker David Jones of neighbouring Pantglas, the extraordinary Italianate palazzo on the southern slopes of Mynydd Llanybydder set in 40 acres of grounds and parkland. Perhaps this Tywi valley exemplar set the standard for an ambitious updating of the gardens at Highmead.

Young Bertie Davies-Evans (1869–1930) grew up in this horticultural hothouse. His diary at the age of eleven recorded his gardening activities in February 1880: 'Planted some radishes to force in the lower vinery and set some potatoes.' Two days later he planted 'some melon and mustard and cress seeds' and caught a rat in the vinery, 'which escaped'.⁶ When he came of age in 1891 a local paper reported that 'the extensive grounds, kept to perfection, put one in mind of the gardens which took so much the fancy of the fabled Aladdin, and give one so much pleasure to loiter in them.'⁷ The gardens must have reached a peak of late-Victorian excellence at this point. Photographs taken in the 1880s show skittles on the terrace, a rustic summer house and boating in elaborate water gardens.

Today Highmead's horticultural fame can be found in the archives rather than on the ground and traces of the panoply of high Victorian garden features must be deliberately sought out. The larger pool with an island seems to have been in place by the mid 19th century, but a second pond and a network of paths appears on the 1889 OS map. An ornamental rock garden was built at the southern end. Today the smaller pond contains not water but garbage. The complex of water features beyond has become true wilderness, with naturalized bamboos *Fargesia spathacea*, *Sasa palmata* and *Sasaella ramosa*, grasses and Himalayan knotweed *Fallopia sacchalinensis* combining with weed trees to conceal collapsed bridges, cascades and rockwork.

To the south of this area lies Highmead's most conspicuous garden relic, the once-splendid productive area contained in a 3.4-acre walled enclosure strategically placed between the mansion and the home farm of Hendy. The main kitchen garden is a grassy paddock, but labelled fruit trees still adorn the walls. There are remains of glasshouses and boiler systems, extensive frameyard, orchard and slip gardens, as well as remnants of woody plants. The 'lower vinery' where young Bertie cut his gardening teeth has disappeared, along with most of the rest of the glasshouse superstructures.

North-west of the water garden, an indeterminate patch of mixed woodland hides the ghost of a feature perhaps unique in Ceredigion gardens: a Victorian maze. OS maps of 1889 and 1905 show an oblong some 25 by 40 yd with a broken rectilinear pattern

Sinuous paths threaded through the Victorian rock garden, all now overgrown.

of inner hedges. The maze is remembered as growing ever more unkempt until it was finally flattened in the epic winter of 1946–7. What it was planted in is not recorded, but scattered clusters of leggy hornbeams that survive in this area suggest that the lost maze was originally delineated by clipped hornbeam hedges.

Major Evans's tree planting made Highmead famous two centuries ago. Some of the interesting specimens existing today in the parkland must date from his successors. Lime trees to the south of the house include *Tilia tomentosa* 'Orbicularis', rare in cultivation outside Kew and Wisley, and *T. x europaea* 'Pallida'.

The decline of the house and its gardens reflects a fate all too common in the 20th century. Even the name Highmead has disappeared from maps of the area since the 1960s.   *P.D.*

[1] Nicholas (1875 edn.) p. 194.

[2] Ibid.

[3] Fenton (1917).

[4] Charles, B.G., 'The Highmead Dairy 1778–97' in *Ceredigion* V, 1 (1964).

[5] NLW MS Highmead 2986.

[6] NLW MS Highmead 81.

[7] NLW MS Highmead 2.

20

Llanerchaeron, Llanaeron

LLANNERCH AERON

The Aeron valley was formed by a much larger river in glacial times. Near the coast the modern river meanders through a broad, fertile alluvial floor, parts of which may have held back a glacial lake. On either side the slopes rise steeply and are clothed in woodland. This favoured spot, two miles inland from Aberaeron and framed by the confluence of the Aeron and its tributary the Mydr, was inhabited in medieval and prehistoric times, as recent excavations at Llanerchaeron have revealed.

A house stood on this site in 1670, when it was the property of John Parry and assessed for hearth tax at six hearths. There is little documentary evidence of its structural history in the following hundred years, during which time it passed by inheritance down the substantial Lewis family and was successively home to the widows Anne Parry and then Elizabeth Lewis (*née* Griffies). By 1867 it had become the home of Elizabeth's son John Lewis and his bride Elizabeth Johnes, of the Carmarthenshire gentry family of Dolaucothi, who reared two sons, Jack and William, and six daughters there. The deaths of Jack in 1775 and of their father in 1789 brought the entire estate into the ownership of the recently married younger son William Lewis.

It is easy to imagine the liberating enthusiasm with which William Lewis and his bride Corbetta Williama Powell (sister of Thomas Powell, squire of Nanteos, with a dowry of £5000) set about building a new home and garden on the site of the old house in about 1791. William Lewis was a young and energetic man, a major in the Cardiganshire Militia, active in local affairs, and on the Cardiganshire Turnpike Trust. In tandem with building his new home, he was instrumental in creating the new road which became the turnpike from Aberaeron to Lampeter, and which was soon to bring a succession of appreciative travellers past his lands. To enhance the impression upon passers-by, he probably also erected the park walls around the setting of his great-grandfather's former home at Ciliau Park, creating the appearance of a deer park recorded on Singer's map of 1803.[1] There is no evidence that deer were ever kept here. He commissioned John Nash, who was then acting as architect on many public projects in Wales as well as on gentry houses, to design him a fashionable new home, and along with it laid out pleasure grounds and walled gardens in the very latest style. He also remodelled the church (almost certainly according to Nash designs) to display a copper dome above a stuccoed tower, framed perfectly in the view from the entrance hall and through the drawing-room windows of the new mansion. In every detail the new Llanaeron mansion, as it was then known, which was completed in 1794, was a mannered expression of the picturesque. Possibly the only landscape traces

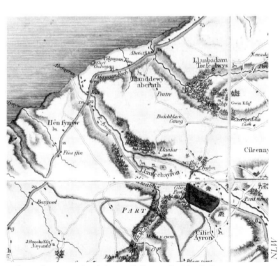

Llanerchaeron, the lake and the park (shaded) on Singer's map of 1803.

of the former house on the site are the hybrid limes *Tilia* x *vulgaris* in the lawn or hay meadow between the mansion and the river Aeron.

The pleasure gardens were laid out to screen the farmstead and walled gardens from view as carriages approached the house, and to lead the pedestrian eastwards from the house towards the newly created lake. Plantings were of beech, frequently bunch-planted, two to a planting hole (as recommended by Humphry Repton) such that, with growth, they would fuse together to make an elegant double-trunked tree. The large-leaved lime *Tilia platyphyllos* has also been bunch-planted in this way. Adjoining the walled garden are 'stoneries', the Georgian precursors of the Victorian rockery. These convex mounds displayed not luxuriant plants but ornamental juxtapositions of stones. At Llanerchaeron the stones used are chiefly white quartzite veins from the lead mines, piddock-bored and sea-smoothed limestone boulders scavenged from Aberaeron beach, and pieces of slag.

The position of the lake, which is identified on Singer's 1803 map, is less felicitous, since it does not compose a vista from anywhere near the mansion, but was probably thus situated because it had been at least in part created by the extraction of clay for the production of bricks for building the house. The field adjoining the lake is labelled on the tithe map Cae Bricks. The lake would, however, have been clearly visible from the new turnpike, as would the new mansion itself.

The walled gardens were the last word in cutting-edge garden technology of the time, with glazed stovehouses leant against heated flue walls through which hot air from small furnaces travelled to chimneys at the top of the wall. The western of the two walled gardens, nearer the house, was particularly lavish, constructed entirely of brick, inside and out, and with buttressing spaced to frame generously espaliered wall plants. The flues

'*View of Llanayron and Church*', as sketched by Mrs Pearson, c. 1842.

here run diagonally as illustrated in design drawings in Miller's *Gardener's Dictionary* 2nd edition (1733). Here the prestigious fruit, vegetables and flowers for the house would have been grown, and their ceremonial importance is emphasized by an entry in William Lewis's diary on 7 July 1822: 'Lord Milford two sons and three daughters were at our church and came to the house and ate some fruit.' This would be Lord Milford of Picton Castle.

The farther, eastern walled garden was of less costly construction, of stone externally instead of brick, and the south wall was probably added at a later date, replacing an earlier hedge. Here, too, there were flues in the thickness of the south-facing north wall, though these appear to run horizontally. The tithe map (1839) shows a substantial rectangular pond, perhaps a stew, within this eastern garden.

The home farm, which adjoins the walled gardens, was built over a period of years and represents an exceptional range of buildings for the self-sufficiency of a small estate.

Two very small square lodges survive, though both now have extensions; Pontfaen Cottage at the eastern junction with the turnpike, and Clwyd Ddu at the western approach. These were probably built in the late 18th century to monitor the roads leading down from the turnpike to the mansion. During William and Corbetta's lifetime, estate

'Mrs Paisey's Cottage' (Abermydr), sketched by Mrs Pearson, c. 1842.

cottages were modified, at least on their roadside faces, to look more designed and picturesque, and Dr Mavor[2] in 1805, having expressed his despair at the dismal ambience of Tregaron, felt his spirits rise as he passed the 'elegant modern seat of Colonel Lewis – standing on a fine plain, where the vale is somewhat more expanded, as if to make room for the embellishments which are here happily applied.' He also remarked upon the picturesque and pleasantly situated peasant dwellings, with whitewashed slate roofs, of the estate. One particularly noteworthy cottage, Abermydr, stands by the river on the western approach. It is octagonal in shape, and although judged to be too crude in design to have been by Nash himself, it may well have been built in imitation of an octagonal ice house design by Nash which had been commissioned by Corbetta's nephew, William Edward Powell of Nanteos.[3] In 1842 it was home to butler Mr Paisey and his wife, and was sketched by a visitor, Mrs Pearson.[4] Beside this cottage stands a vast and shapely London plane *Platanus* x *hispanica*. This is the largest of just seven in the county; the others are planted in the pleasure grounds of Nanteos, Llanllŷr, Highmead, Falcondale, Brynog and near Aberllolwyn. Like Powell of Nanteos, William Lewis's records show that he bought plants from Miller of Bristol, Nurseryman.

The second significant owner of Llanaeron was John Lewis, their son, who, after a rakish youth, married at the age of 48. His bride, Mary Ashby Mettam, a clergyman's daughter of good family from Leicestershire, was 20 years his junior. The marriage was childless. John's structural contributions to the estate included a handsome billiard room (1843) thought to be by architect W.R. Coulthart[5], which stands separate from the house, and the addition of a bay window (1855) to the morning room in which he sat. (This has recently been removed by the National Trust.) In 1852 he had also harnessed the water from the lake to a waterwheel which drove machinery in the large barn. The water was taken in a leat under the eastern walled garden, and its cobble-lined dipping wells may have been installed at the same time. New ornamental trees on the lake shore, cedar of Lebanon and wellingtonia, mark the bank repair around the newly constructed outlet.

John Lewis's death in 1855 left Mary Ashby Lewis in possession of Llanaeron for 62 years until her death at the age of 104 in 1917. It seems that a sitting widow is good for garden conservation. During Mary's custodianship her reputation was one of a benevolent autocrat who took a close interest in her staff. In 1863 a bailiff-cum-gardener's house was erected for Thomas Baynton and his wife rising above the north wall of the western walled garden, with windows strategically placed to supervise both farm and garden. In the western walled garden new greenhouses with hot-water central-heating pipes fed by boilers replaced the Georgian stovehouses. A brick-lined dipping well was installed and both this and the eastern well were edged with glistening white quartzite blocks. Garden flowers were purchased from the Royal Nurseries, Slough, and ferns from Tenby.

Like a true Victorian, Mary Lewis kept swans upon her lake and ornamental pheasants (purchased from W. Chamberlain in 1873) in an aviary, possibly in the north-west corner of the west walled garden. She also stocked a pheasantry in the hanging woods on the north side of the Aeron and constructed the circuit walk in Lanlâs wood linked by footbridges to the mansion on the south side of the river. One of her last projects was the so-called Dutch Garden outside the west walled garden, which is recollected by John Morgan, who came to work at Llanerchaeron in 1928, as very pretty with flower beds, mown grass and a little circular pond. As with the pools in the walled gardens, this was edged with white quartzite. She was a very old lady when the railway came, cutting across the far margin of the Regency lawn. While allowing this development, she ensured that a halt was built from which groceries could be delivered directly to the house.

It was a great-nephew, Capt. T.P. Lewes (who had formerly rented both Cwmcoedwig and Abermâd), who eventually inherited Llanerchaeron and the debts which encumbered it. Capt. and Mrs T.P. Lewes were amiable gentlefolk who supported the local hospital and the local hunt. A remnant of their gardening interest is the box-edged rose parterre which has been recently reconstructed in the warm north-west corner of the walled garden, where the aviary probably formerly stood. In their tenure the water power was adapted to charge batteries for electric lighting in the mansion. The house then passed to their son, John Powell Ponsonby Lewes, who became increasingly reclusive in his lifetime, and left the estate to the National Trust. Although his staff were few, the walled gardens had never been abandoned, and thanks to the timely formation of a group of gardening volunteers while the legal processes were still underway, it escaped destruction by rank weeds and brambles. Among the features in the west walled garden today are a rare survivor of the 1950s, a concrete greenhouse by the Hendy Quarry Co. Ltd of Pontyclun, Glamorgan, and three restored late 19th-century heated glasshouses, one of which is identified as a No. 52 Span-roof Villa Greenhouse made by the Norwich firm of Boulton and Paul. The mansion has been restored and it is expected that the silted and overgrown lake will soon be reinstated.

For information about regular opening times and special events out of season, contact the National Trust.   *C.P.*

[1] Singer, J., A New Map of Cardiganshire (1803).
[2] Mavor (1809).
[3] Suggett, R., *John Nash Architect in Wales*, Aberystwyth (1995).
[4] Sketch book by Mrs Pearson 1842-55. NLW Drawing Vol. 70.
[5] Palmer, C. & Laidlaw, R., 'William Ritson Coulthart and the Llanerchaeron Billiard Room', in *Ceredigion* XIII, 3, pp. 43–6 (1999).

Also see:
Evans, M.L., *Llanerchaeron*, Y Lolfa (1996).
Palmer, C.D. and Laidlaw, R., Historic Landscape Survey, Llanerchaeron. Report to the National Trust, (1999).

CDP 1998

Llanerchaeron: espaliered apples in the west walled garden.

21

Llanllŷr, Llanllear
LLANFIHANGEL YSTRAD

Llanllŷr represents a rarity in the Ceredigion landscape – a house standing amid extensive level ground rather than nestling into the irregularities of a 'picturesque' setting. As the Aeron turns through a generous right-angle to flow from south- to north-westwards, it has scoured a wider than usual area of valley bottom – probably one of the largest inland areas of river plain in the county. Over recent centuries the river and its tributaries have been locally channelled and the land drained into pasture. In 1896 Col. John Lewes estimated that the course of the Aeron had been straightened between 1750 and 1790. Capt. J. Hext Lewes in 1971 suggested a far earlier date – that the stretch from Talsarn Bridge down to Brynog might have been dug as early as the 1650s.[1] In these fertile green acres sits Llanllŷr house and farm, its modest park and four-acre gardens. The austere building and its tree-studded parkland can be glimpsed from the B4337. Another marker is the lodge (listed grade II) to the north of the property, near Talsarn bridge.

Llanllŷr is also unusual for Ceredigion in that some kind of gardening must have been continuous on this site for over eight centuries, and the garden is thriving today. A chapel may predate the small Cistercian nunnery established here by the Lord Rhys in 1180 as a daughter house of the monastery at Strata Florida. No trace remains, but the white nuns of 'Llan Clere' mentioned by Leland

Thomas Dineley's sketch c. 1684.

presumably followed the well-established Cistercian traditions of orderly, utilitarian horticulture. Some three centuries later Meyrick found that the 'venerable retired spot' still filled his mind with 'reverend awe', and found pleasure in contemplating 'the haunt of those holy females', although he rejoiced at the light of the Reformation. He made no mention of the grounds other than to note that a corpse in a leaden coffin was dug up in the garden 'a few years back'.

Towards the end of the 16th century the Lloyd family, into whose possession Llanllŷr passed after the Dissolution of 1536, replaced the nunnery with a house. There were marriages with the Pryse family of Gogerddan, the Lloyds of Llanfair Clydogau and Richard 2nd Earl of Carbery, but as the owners sank deeply into debt and mortgage the financial history of Llanllŷr in the later 17th century is turbulent. The house was assessed at six hearths in 1672 and was described in 1694 as a decayed house in the hands of a tenant. Thomas Dineley's stylized drawing of 1684[2] presumed to depict Llanllŷr (the original bears the Lloyd coat of arms) shows a two-and three-storey Tudor house with a formal garden layout which can be interpreted as corresponding to a map of 1768. This estate map of 'Llanllear Demesne' shows a large formal garden of two walled compartments to the east of the Tudor house.

Today's owners are descended from John Lewes (1680–1742) of Llysnewydd, on the Carmarthenshire bank of the Teifi near Henllan, who bought Llanllŷr in 1720 from the heir of Henry Sumner, to whom Llanllŷr had been mortgaged in 1662. John Lewes was a merchant, mayor of Carmarthen in 1724 and of Cardigan in 1731 and 1736, and High Sheriff of Cardiganshire in 1730. John Lewes's son, John Lewes II (1711–83), inherited Llysnewydd on the death of his cousin in 1728, so Llanllŷr remained a tenanted farmhouse until 1826. Then Capt. John Lewes (1793–1860), who had fought at Waterloo, married Mary Anne Lloyd (1802–42) of Brynog. 'Waterloo' Lewes was given Llanllŷr as his marriage portion and decided to live there. Improvements became necessary.

The Tudor house was demolished in about 1830. Its materials were used to build the replacement, supplemented by bricks baked near by. During the rebuilding part of an Early Christian pillar stone with incised crosses and a latin inscription was found. It is now displayed as a garden feature (see overleaf). The house was further enlarged around 1870, thanks to the wealth of Mary Jane Griffiths of Llwyndyrys, who had married Col. John Lewes (1828–1900) in 1858, and in order to accommodate their nine children. There have been two generations of owners since then, and there are two further generations of potential owners to date.

The framework of today's pleasure gardens and parkland is based on the early 19th-century layout, although the route of the main drive was slightly altered in the 20th century. OS maps of 1886 and 1905 show much the same footprint, but a greater number of specimen trees. Today the park is divided into large pasture fields, studded with oaks, conifers and unusual Huntingdon elms *Ulmus* x *vegeta*. A specimen Japanese elm *U. japonica* stands in the field to the north-east of the house.

The unusual kitchen garden surrounded by well-preserved cob walls rendered and

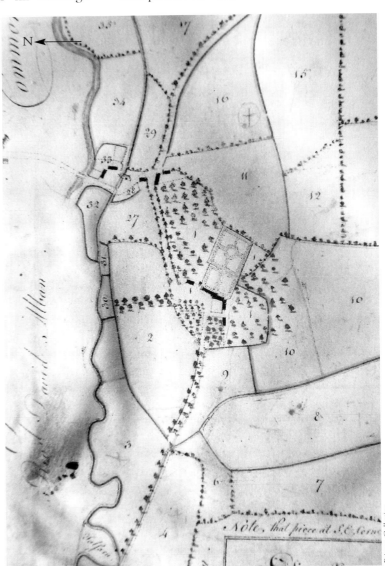

Private Collection

Detail from the 1768 estate map of 'Llanllear Demesne' showing formal gardens to the east of the Tudor house.

Llanllŷr: the remnant of the Early Christian pillar stone found when the house was rebuilt in about 1830 is now displayed in the garden.

garden was in place by 1886. These areas were neglected and overgrown when the present owners, Mr and Mrs Robert Gee, took the gardens in hand in the 1980s. At first they embarked on a creative and far-reaching programme of renewal and regeneration within the existing framework. The shrubbery was replanted and the old rose garden replaced with shrub rose borders designed with the help of Hazel le Rougetel. Box-edged knots in the lee of the house have been wittily designed to reflect the iconography of the original Tudor or Jacobean garden. Gradually new features have been added to extend the ornamental gardens into the wider pleasure grounds – an informal pool and bog garden, a formal sunken water garden, an arbour, a labyrinth, all exhibiting fine plantsmanship. Here is splendid, ambitious gardening taking Llanllŷr into a new millennium.

Llanllŷr opens occasionally for the National Gardens Scheme.   *P.D.*

[1] *Archaeologia Cambrensis* (1896) p. 124, and 'Llanllŷr 1180–1980' in *Ceredigion* VI 4 (1971) p. 345.
[2] Dineley (1888), p. LXXI.

protected with pitched tiled roofs is probably part of the 1830s development. A plan of it was drawn in 1860, indicating the position of fruit trees and accompanied by notes on their productivity. Today parts of the original path system remain, with some espaliered and wall-trained fruit trees.

The ornamental gardens lie to the east and south of the house. The main path arrangement in the 'shrubbery', in the angle between the house and the kitchen garden, is original and must date to the 1830 rebuilding. The rose border layout paralleling the kitchen

The approach to the rebuilt house in the early 1900s.

Llidiardau

LLANILAR

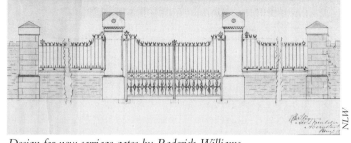

Design for new carriage gates by Roderick Williams of Aberystwyth, 1876.

Llidiardau stands on the southern flank of the Ystwyth valley between Llanilar and Trawsgoed. It was bought, along with the adjoining home farm and 124 acres, by David Parry in 1739. By the late 18th century it was the home of his son Thomas Parry, JP and Deputy Lieutenant of the county, his wife (sister of John Williams of Castle Hill) and his family of five daughters and a son. This was a gentry family whose daughters' social life was severely constrained by their possessive father, but much enlivened by the lasting friendships formed with Jane Johnes and her daughter Mariamne, as a result of their three-year residence at neighbouring Castle Hill.[1]

The tithe map of 1845 reflects the gentrification of this small mansion, for it is described as 'house and parterre', an unusually specific term. Probably this reflects not only a formal lawned platform, but the fact that that platform was of made ground, giving an uninterrupted view up the valley to the east. Below this platform, and on the opposite side of the road, were two fields managed as lawn or hay meadow, while the steep slopes behind the house were wooded, and had been extended eastward with a tree nursery and two newer plantations in the former fields. As at Hafod, planting was of larch and oak. The house was a compact boxy structure which faced south-east and was adjoined to the north-west by farm buildings and 'hayguard'. Both were approached directly from the road below, and a small area described as orchard and garden occupied a triangular plot to the left of the entrance.

The whole layout was radically remodelled in 1854 by the architect Richard Kyrke Penson for Thomas Parry's great-grandson George Williams Parry III. The old house seems to have been demolished, and a new one constructed on the site of the farm buildings. A narrow cottage behind the new house may be the only remaining trace of the old farm. A new home farm and coach house were constructed on the site of the former orchard and garden below, and a new walled garden and orchard on the slope behind the house. There may always have been some access from the road through the strip of woodland to the north-west, but now this became the main drive, entirely separating the visitor from the utilitarian parts of the estate. Some very handsome gates by the builder Roderick Williams of Aberystwyth were designed for this entrance in 1876.[2]

By the 1950s this drive had entirely disappeared into an impenetrable thicket of rhododendrons, and was rescued by new owners, who also obtained and erected the station waiting room from Llanilar as a garden building west of the house. Several large oaks margin the route, but the most unexpected tree on the site is a single Lombardy poplar *Populus nigra* 'Plantierensis', which stands alone, some 18m tall, west of the walled garden.

The site of the old house is now a croquet lawn, and the garden contains some very fine trees, shrubs and borders introduced by the present owners. In the spirit of innovation, they have constructed a stone-built folly attached to the orchard wall.

[1] Barber, J., '"Most Flattering to his feelings": Thomas Johnes of Hafod and the Cardiganshire Gentry' in *NLW Journal*, XXVIII (1994), pp. 391–404.
[2] NLW Llidiardau 30, 31.

Lodge Park, Bodvage
LLANGYNFELYN

The road from Talybont to Machynlleth skirts the hills, and affords fine views westward over Borth bog and the Dyfi estuary. Three miles north of Talybont the outlook is blocked by an island of high ground, clad in birch woodland, and at the apex of this hill, exposed to every wind, stands the house known as Lodge Park.

The principal importance of this site is for its deer park, a lozenge-shaped enclosure of about 100 acres which encloses this hill, and may well be the only medieval deer park in the county. It first appears in the written record in 1637 in a lease of Park Bodvage (Lodge Park) granted by Richard Pryse of Gogerddan who reserved to himself and his heirs 'the pasture of three horses, nags geldings or mares at all times during the said terme within the said parke, and common of pasture for his and their deare [deer] within the said parke, with free access egresse and regresse thereunto to hunt course chase or kill the same at his or their pleasure…'[1] Lodge Park had long been a part of the estate of Gogerddan, whose earliest recorded owner was Rhydderch ap Ieuan Lloyd the celebrated poet, himself a descendant of Cadivor ap Gwaethvoed, Lord of Cardigan, from whom the Pryses of Gogerddan claimed descent.[2] A connection with Rhydderch could

place the park's origins in the 12th or 13th century, when most of the large English estates established deer parks of similar form and dimensions.

The characteristic feature of a medieval deer park is its shape, defined by the 'park pale', a fence or hedge on top of a bank-and-ditch earthwork. At the highest point within the park a functional building, the park lodge, would provide a workplace for the parkers. The park was not so much a hunting and recreational place as a source of venison, firewood and timber. Most parks were stocked with fallow deer.[3]

The boundary of the park is still discernible along the north and west margins. Particularly distinctive are the walls at the north-east boundary in which the internal ditch is enclosed by an earth bank revetted with upright slabs of stone. This construction is also found to the west of the A487 where a series of three small fields runs south of the park. A

The outer bank of the deer park wall at the north-east boundary of the park.

CDP 1997

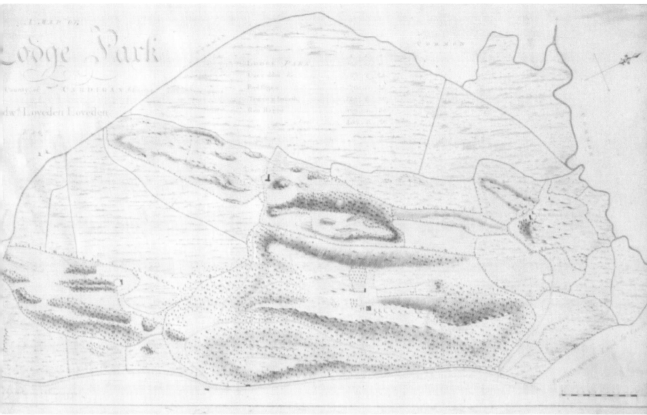

'A Map of Lodge Park belonging to Edward Loveden Loveden by T. Lewis. Surveyed 1779' shows fields, woods and reclaimed marsh adjoining the old deer park. NLW map 7142.

more traditional dry-stone wall marks the eastern boundary of the park. This, however, is probably only a couple of hundred years old, for by 1779 the turnpike road took a new route, cutting off the eastern quarter of the old park, which became known as Ergid y Bwa (bowshot) wood.[4] Just inside the 18th-century wall are a number of large small-leaved limes *Tilia cordata*. There are a few very venerable oaks near the north margin and within the park, and a very large suckering stump of an unusual clone of hybrid lime *Tilia x vulgaris* inside the north-east margin of the park. Most late 17th- and early 18th-century hybrid limes in parks and gardens belong to just two clonal groups originating in the Netherlands. The interest is that this tree, which more closely resembled the species *T. platyphyllos*, belongs to

neither of these clones.[5]

By the 17th century the parkers' lodge had been replaced by a more substantial house, successively leased to Hugh Myddleton of Chirk Castle (1620–31), and later to Thomas Bushell (1637–42). Both these men were engaged in exploiting the newly discovered mineral wealth of Cardiganshire, and the adits and shafts within Lodge Park probably date from Bushell's time. There is a rock-cut spring holding a pool of clear water some 18in deep part way down the north-facing slope of the park at some distance from the house. It is known as Bushell's well, and may according to oral history be where Bushell is alleged to have drowned his wife or maidservant. In the survey of 1779 the house is shown to be adjoined by two enclosed areas, one a garden and orchard,

Lodge Park in the late 19th century. Photo Album 1080. The oak in the foreground has since been replaced by a specimen Picea smitheana.

the other perhaps a paddock, and flanked by a line of trees on the eastern escarpment. Deerkeeping had probably ceased, and the house was leased or used to accommodate younger scions of the Pryse family. It was substantially enlarged and rebuilt in 1787–91. To the north of the house are various outbuildings enumerated in 1805 as stable, barn, 'cowtying' and granary.[6] The walled kitchen garden is probably contemporaneous with this phase of rebuilding, and the property was now described in a valuation as a desirable Residence for a Gentleman's family. Dr Mavor described the residence in glowing terms in 1809:

> Having heard much of the beauty of Lodge Park … we proceeded to visit it. A broad winding path through a wood … conducts to the house, which stands on a bold eminence and commands some of the finest views in the world. It is astonishing that such a delightful spot has not been more frequently visited by travellers. In this park are some valuable mines, and in particular one, which has produced a considerable quantity of silver within the last thirty years.

The garden associated with the house today is largely of Victorian planting. Lodge Park was home to Pryse Loveden and then to his widow

Margaretta Jane and her second husband, H. C. Fryer. It was described by Nicholas in 1872 as 'a delightfully situated residence commanding an extensive prospect of land and sea surrounded by sylvan scenes and tastefully ornamented grounds.' Specimen trees to the south of the mansion include wellingtonia, monkey puzzle, *Thuja plicata*, *Cryptomeria japonica*, Irish yew and the largest Douglas fir (girth 528cm) in Ceredigion. The undergrowth is of rhododendron and cherry laurel, and concealed within it is a circular cairn-style rockery of white quartzite boulders. The plinths of two Victorian summerhouses are situated on a ridge commanding views to the west.

The old deer park is on Forest Commission land and may be explored on foot. The mansion itself is a private home.   *C.P.*

[1] NLW MS Gogerddan 280.
[2] Meyrick (1810).
[3] Rackham, O., *The History of the Countryside* London (1986).
[4] NLW MS Maps Vol. 37.
[5] Pigott, D., *New Phytology* 121, 1992, pp. 487–93, and A.O. Chater, pers. comm.
[6] NLW MS Gogerddan. Particulars of valuations of farms 1805.

Nanteos
LLANFIHANGEL-Y-CREUDDYN

The Nant Paith drains the high ground which separates the broad valleys of the Rheidol and Ystwyth rivers, both of which reach the sea at Aberystwyth. Two miles upstream from its confluence with the Ystwyth, the Paith valley has a broad floor, and it is here, at the foot of wooded slopes and enjoying a fine south-facing prospect, that Nanteos mansion is situated.

One of the four really big estates in the county, Nanteos lands extended to 30,000 acres in the late 18th and early 19th centuries. The setting of the house today principally reflects the Regency style of Col. William Edward Powell, a young man who came into his estates aged 21 in 1810 and promptly married Laura Phelp, a young English woman of good family and little fortune, well supplied with younger siblings. Laura Place in Aberystwyth is named after her, though recent linguistic reform has relabelled it Maes Lowri.

Despite very real and pressing financial problems, improvements were immediately undertaken. Since he had lost his father at the age of eleven, Nanteos had been rented out, and the house he inherited was both unfashionable and in poor repair. Powell required a home commensurate with his ambitions, which soon were to encompass High

Sheriff, Lord Lieutenant of the county, and MP. Like other landowners in Cardiganshire, his father Thomas Powell had embraced the opportunities offered by the turnpike trust to improve his privacy by rerouting the public road further from his front door. Had he lived longer he might perhaps have implemented the lavish picturesque landscape design which he had commissioned from John Davenport in 1791, and which would have embellished the demesne with a fine assortment of temples, rotundas, ruins, castles and towers. As it turned out, other hands and minds redesigned the Nanteos grounds in the 19th century.

William Edward Powell's improvements spanned 35 years. They began with a remodelled front apron to the house, a greenhouse west of the house and proposals for a flower garden east of the kitchen garden, and led on to the construction of the exceptionally grand stable block with classical arched entrance screen, the walling of the kitchen garden, the creation of the lake and new

Nanteos as depicted in Meyrick (1810).

plantations and shrubberies. A bill from Miller's nursery in Bristol in 1832 included copper beech, cherry laurel, Portugal laurel, evergreen oak, Weymouth pine, lilac, laburnum, flowering currant, double sweet briar, evergreen sweet briar, moss rose and various herbaceous plants and bulbs. Some of these trees are almost certainly the specimens seen today in the former shrubbery south of the walled garden.

Fine surviving trees from this period include a cedar of Lebanon, several ginkgos (one of which is the largest in the county), holm oak, silver fir, copper beech and common beech. A very large tulip tree near the south wall of the flower garden (rumoured to be the hiding place of buried Powell jewels) is now a rotting stump with suckering regrowth. The walls of the kitchen garden are brick-lined on the south- and east-facing walls to provide the best microclimate for fruit cultivation. Remnants of the melon house, vinery and sheds and frames remain in the now overgrown walled garden. Gardeners' records of 1842–44 show that every month excess produce was sold from the garden. The cost of a melon, at 2/-, shows the prestige of such horticulture, for this is a sum equivalent to a week's wages for a woman weeding the garden. Over the year surpluses were sold of seakale, broccoli, leeks, carrots, cucumbers, asparagus, rhubarb, lettuce, gooseberries, peas, cauliflower, potatoes, strawberries, cherries, beans, cabbage, artichokes, raspberries, blackcurrants, melons, apples, pears, damsons and onions. Recently, large stretches of the walls on the southern margin have leant, bowed and eventually collapsed, and Japanese knotweed is creating impenetrable thickets around the old melon house.

There are also the traces of the earlier landscape style associated with the 18th century. The boxy Palladian central block of Nanteos mansion was built in 1739, on the site of the previous house of the Joneses of Nanteos, and perhaps also incorporated materials such as window headers from Llechwedd Dyrys, the Powells' former family house on the opposite side of the valley, which by 1764 had been demolished. Small dry-stone footbridges allowed the visitor to cross the stream and climb the facing slope to visit the eyecatcher façade which faced the mansion from across the valley of the Paith. From there, the sea can be glimpsed as a brilliant triangle of blue to the west, and the 18th-century visitor might also have admired the hounds confined in a kennel enclosure behind the façade. The façade is ruined now, though both ends and

The 18th-century eyecatcher façade which concealed the kennels. In 1788 the public road ran close by.

part of the blind Venetian window at the west end survive. Looking back across the lawn or park, punctuated by ancient oaks, the visitor would have seen a triangular, fenced pleasure ground, extending westward from the house.

Rounded clumps of beech trees on the slope east of the eyecatcher were planted early in the 19th century and show the influence of Humphry Repton's landscape ideas. In the Nanteos archive are elevations and plans for alterations to the mansion, and for lodges, dairy and icehouse, a keeper's cottage and a garden house drawn by George Repton (son of Humphry) who was working in the office of

John Nash at that time. The designs were commissioned in 1810–11 by John Edwards, an attorney and cousin of Nash, who was acting as William Edward Powell's agent in setting the estate in order after the years of tenancy and neglect. Only one of these designs, the lodge on the western approach, appears to have been completed, although the mason's accounts show that an icehouse was being constructed in 1831. A second icehouse, by W.R. Coulthart, was designed in 1841, in conjunction with plans for the east wing of the mansion.

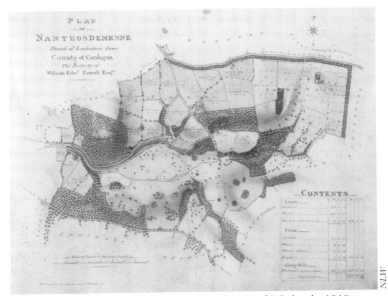

Estate survey by land surveyor William Crawford Jr. of Edinburgh, 1819.

When Powell eventually died in 1854, aged 66, his son William Thomas Rowland Powell inherited and, aided by his cousin and agent William Edward Phelp, ran the estate for the next 24 years. The Nash lodge was replaced in 1857 by the present Italianate lodge designed by local architect Richard Kyrke Penson, and a billiard room was appended to the east wing. The estate was managed for sport, and pheasant shoots, otter-hunting and foxhunting at Nanteos feature large in the sketches of W.T.R. Powell and the published reminiscences of Col. Newton Wynne Apperley.[1] Ornamental gardening was not, however, neglected: plant orders to Hale Farm, Tottenham, were for roses and verbenas, and to

Specimen beeches south-east of the mansion.

Newton Nursery, Chester, for gladioli. A huge and cumulative bill from James Veitch, the Royal Exotic Nursery, Kings Road, Chelsea, was for £153 17s 3d. Probably Veitch had supplied the wellingtonias *Sequoiadendron giganteum* which were by then being planted in the old pleasure ground and in Penglanowen wood, and the greenhouses and frames which can be seen in the 1st edition 25-inch OS survey of the walled garden. W.T.R. Powell, father of the aesthete George, entertained lavishly at Nanteos, and it is pleasing to read the press description of the flaming torches illuminating the long drive as his guests attended his fancy dress ball in 1875.

The later owners of Nanteos made few alterations to its grounds, and although much has been lost, there remains the tranquil atmosphere of a Regency demesne.   *C.P.*

[1] Apperley, Newton Wynne, *A Hunting Diary*, London (1926).

Also see:
Palmer, C.D., 'Soaring Ambitions in the Nanteos Demesne' in Gerald Morgan (ed.), *Nanteos – A Welsh House and its Families*, Llandysul (2001).

25

National Library of Wales

LLANBADARN FAWR

The gardens of the National Library of Wales have, in conjunction with the other 20th-century campus grounds on the slopes of Penglais Hill, been designated grade II★ in the *Register*. The NLW, commenced in 1911, is by several decades the earliest and perhaps the most ostentatiously planned of these public areas. The design for the National Library was chosen by competition amongst architects, and Sidney Greenslade's concept for the site verged upon the baroque: a handsome quadrangular library, enfolding a central dome and set about by ornate satellite buildings on either side, the Librarian's house, the lecture theatre, the lodge,

and a smaller domed heating and refreshment block. The site would be approached from below, up elaborate flights of steps and landings ornamented with ornate lamps and statuary. The living components of this landscape would have been confined to formal lawns and close-mown grass, the whole having something of the formality of a French château about it.

Interrupted by World War I, and held back by Greenslade's bouts of depression, the execution and the aesthetic of the NLW underwent substantial modification as the project progressed. For more than 20 years the two reading rooms rose from amongst staff allotments and a building site and loomed like twin shoe boxes above the town. When the central administration block was built in 1934 the architect was Charles Holden and his drawings, although influenced by the Greenslade plan, involved much sparer, almost

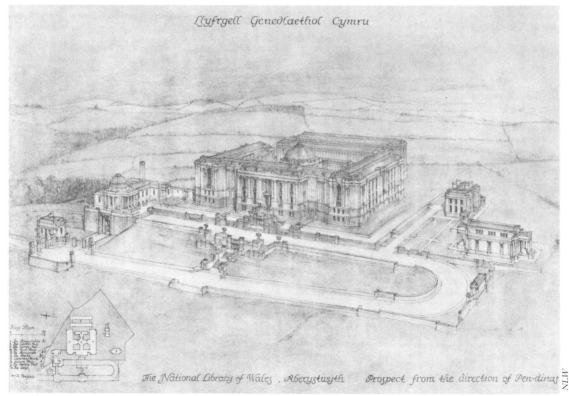

Llyfrgell Genedlaethol Cymru

The National Library of Wales, Aberystwyth   Prospect from the direction of Pen-dinas

Sidney Greenslade's prizewinning design for the site.

Bauhaus design. This is particularly true of the approaching steps and terraces, built of monumental granite block, and ornamented with very stylish art deco standard lamps. Holden's treatment of the terraces introduced flower beds at the level of the entrance terrace, and a simple sloping lawned bed at the foot

Postcard, 1931, showing the two reading rooms before construction of the central block.

of this wall. The first actual planting of these terraces in 1937, in anticipation of the royal vist of King George VI and Queen Elizabeth, seems to have been less minimalist than Holden envisaged and involved regularly spaced yews (perhaps destined for topiary) on the upper terrace, and roses and fuchsias rather than lawn in the beds below.

Also established at this time was the extensive rockery which flanks the approach to the library between the 1930s vernacular lodge and the formal lawns, and continues as a margin along its lower edge. This is notable for the use of a locally fabricated rockery stone, a concrete composite in which smooth river pebbles, sharp fragments and pieces of brick have been mixed in a pale-coloured cement of very stiff consistency, to create an artificial conglomerate typified by voids within its structure. The rockery was cut by winding footpaths and in early days was planted with oriental poppies, alyssum and agapanthus. In 1948

The Robin Urn from Mariamne's garden at Hafod stood in the Library gardens in the 1970s.

it was embellished by the Carrara marble urn by Thomas Banks which had formerly been the focal point of Mariamne's garden at Hafod. This was removed for safekeeping in the 1980s, and is now in the library's new atrium. The rockery is now well established with a good range of ornamental shrubs and perennial plants.

The yews on the terrace probably did not flourish under the influence of salt-laden winds, and by the 1960s were replaced by the regularly spaced *Euonymus japonicus* bushes which now punctuate the upper terrace, the approach drive and the footpath leaving the site. A mixture of roses, fuchsias and bedding plants is still grown in the terrace flowerbeds, but the most striking features are the euonymus balls and the well-established clumps of nerines which produce gleaming beacons of pink every October.

The new Pendinas Restaurant is now approached through the side entrance on the south-west front and parts of the terrace have been slate-paved in the modern patio style. Sadly, the euonymus balls in this area have been severely pruned to a rectangular shape. *C.P.*

Also see:
Huws, D., *The National Library of Wales - A history of the Building*, Aberystwyth (1994).
Palmer, C.D., in *Cyfaill y Llyfrgell/ Friend of the Library*, Winter 2003, pp. 12–16.

26

Penglais, Penglaise
LLANBADARN FAWR, VAINOR ISSA

The Penglais estate formerly encompassed much land to the north of Aberystwyth, with woods and pastures but very little prime valley-bottom land. The house is on the flank of Penglais hill, facing south, and sheltered from the salt-laden winds which drive in over the town from the sea.

An inventory of 1746 shows there was a significant house at Penglais which is believed to have been built in 1696 by Roderick Richardes, whose ancestors, (formerly known as Rhydderch) once owned substantial amounts of land in the Rheidol valley. His great-grandson, also Roderick, served with Richard Morris of Anglesey in the Navy Office, London, and retired to Penglais to build a fashionable new mansion and to serve as High Sheriff in 1770. He died in 1785 but was survived by his widow Mary until 1808. As a result, the estate skipped a generation and passed directly to his grandson Roderick Eardley Richardes, eldest of four children brought up at Warden Court, Presteigne, Radnorshire.[1] This Roderick has gained posthumous notoriety as a result of personal letters in the Nanteos archive as Aberystwyth's most prominent blackguard.[2] Other researchers view him in a much less jaundiced light. Notwithstanding the indications of debt and domestic violence, his marriage to Anna Corbetta Powell, a Nanteos heiress, was productive of seven children (born between 1821 and 1836), and though by 1843 the Richardeses were living separately, the marriage was not dissolved until 1848. Two of Roderick Richardes's brothers had also installed themselves in significant houses in the Aberystwyth area: William Eardley Richardes at Bryneithin, and Col. Thomas Charles Richardes at Aberllolwyn.

In 1871 the Penglais estate still extended to 1600 acres. It passed, diminishing, down two further generations of Richardes before the extinction of the line in World War I and the death of Roderick Clement Richardes in 1925. The National Library of Wales and the University of Wales Aberystwyth campus are built upon former Richardes land.

A watercolour shows the new mansion, perched on an apron of made ground.[3] A narrow terrace ran west of it, backed by a plant-wall and terminating in an arched alcove facing the house. This alcove and terrace survives today, but there is no longer any trace of the elegant quartered garden on the south-facing slope behind it. Shelter belts of trees protected the garden from east and west, but the artist depicts bare hills rather than the plantations which later clothed the hillside.

The tithe map of 1845 shows an east-west strand of plantations, and the new mansion handsomely situated on its platform at the foot of the woods. Beyond it is a second building which is thought to be the old Penglais. The plantations behind the house contained a well-engineered track stretching westward to the seaward flank of Penglais hill and descending the hill to the town near the North Gate. To the south, in front of the house, were two meadows, the upper and the lower lawns, which sloped down to the stream, and were managed for hay, as was a further field, 'the house field', behind the mansion. Such ornamental garden as then existed was probably confined to the house platform and the terrace. Of the former enclosed garden the tithe map shows no trace. Produce gardens were in two small fields adjoining the entrance from the road up Penglais hill.

Notwithstanding the stormy financial and family life of Roderick Eardley Richardes and Anna Corbetta, it seems that she and her young children have been the most significant influence upon the garden landscape at Penglais. It is known that the house was extensively remodelled in 1842–43 and that at that time Anna Corbetta and her family were in residence, while her estranged husband paid the bills. She, in conjunction with her younger children, incorporated the dingle into the garden, planting oaks, beeches and hybrid lime trees and building paths which explored its length, crossing and recrossing the stream on four neat single-arch stone bridges. The western of these bridges bears a square slate plaque reading: This Bridge & Railings were Planed by AVARINA W. A. RICHARDS in 1844. The next bridge bears a similar plaque, bearing the same spelling mistakes, and the name of

'Plas Penglaise the seat of Rodrk Richardes Esq.' c. 1790-1800.

CHARLES RICHARDS 1844. Two other bridges crossed the dingle upstream of the drive. One has collapsed, but the upper bridge also bears an identical plaque in the name of Avarina and on this bridge the railings, surmounted by iron urn finials, survive. In 1844 Charles was fourteen years of age and Avarina nine: possibly they are the youngest historic garden designers in Cardiganshire. The dingle today is neglected, but limes mark the corners of Charles's bridge and naturalized clumps of large double snowdrops, similar to those at Nanteos, still flourish among the carpet of ivy.

Anna Corbetta was also innovating on behalf of her family in the woods behind the mansion. The viewpoint from the woodland path behind the mansion is protected by railings with urn finials like those on the bridges. Near by are naturalized old double daffodils and double snowdrops, both cultivars characteristic of old gardens. Further west, three former small fields adjoining the

Old double daffodils at Penglais, attributable as Narcissus pseudonarcissus 'Van Sion' but for a greenish hue reminiscent of the Derwydd daffodil.

plantation were planted with a pure stand of beech trees to create a continuous woodland walk from Penglais to the oak woodland on the western flank of Penglais hill. Here a very substantial 'cottage' was built in a commanding position overlooking the town of Aberystwyth and the sea. By the census of 1851 this was home to her eldest son Alexander Richardes, his first wife Elizabeth and three young children. His household was that of a gentleman, and included three house servants. It is tantalizing that there are no known images of it.

Alexander inherited on the death of his mother in 1860 and lived at Penglais for almost twenty years before leaving his adult children in possession of the mansion, and moving back to Penglaise Cottage with his teenage third wife and baby. He died in 1883.

The 25-inch OS map of 1885 shows that by then the entire length of the dingle was bordered by woodland, and an entrance lodge had been built in the southern of the two former produce gardens. The drive crosses the stream on a causeway with a single gothic stone arch. Remnant structures in the stream suggest a waterwheel may have been installed, perhaps to generate electricity. Above the drive a sluice held back a pool around which skirted an ornamental path. Near by is a large cork oak *Quercus suber*, a tree rare in Wales and unique in this county.[5]

By 1904 much land had been disposed of and the bottom of the dingle garden, adjoining what is now Dan-y-coed, had become a public park known as Elysian Grove in which an outdoor stage displayed pierrots, nigger minstrels, and competitions for singing whilst holding a live pig.[6] In wet weather entertainments were staged in a wooden hut, the Sylvan Palace, which was also used for auction sales.

In 1946 the dilapidated mansion and 25 acres of grounds were acquired and refurbished

Charles Richardes's bridge in the lower dingle, Penglais, and the plaque on Avarina's bridge downstream.

as the residence for the Principal of the University College of Wales. A tennis court was built north of the dingle and a croquet lawn in front of the house. The neglected gardens were rejuvenated and planted by the botany department. Some unusual trees including medlar, *Cedrus atlantica glauca*, *Liriodendron tulipifera*, *Nothofagus dombeyi*, *Laburnum alpinum* and *Parrotia persica* were introduced. Rhododendrons and azaleas were planted near the drive and large-leafed rhododendrons and a few camellias in the dingle. The old terrace

extending west of the mansion was embellished with a small formal slate-edged lily pond. In the 1950s the lawns to the south-west of the mansion were planted as botanical order beds, in which island beds contained related genera of plants, rising from the most primitive such as the magnolias and buttercups at the bottom of the slope to the most evolutionarily recent at the top. These beds were maintained for around 30 years, but underfunding and the reduced emphasis on taxonomy in botany degree courses led to their neglect. The juxtaposition of some well-grown and rather unusual shrubs and trees in this area is consequent upon this period in its history.   *C.P.*

[1] Potter, Coralie Sian, 1990, NLW manuscript EX 986.
[2] Colyer, R.J., 'Roderick Eardley Richardes and Plas Penglais Aberystwyth' in *Ceredigion* X (1981), pp. 99–103.
[3] NLW pictures and maps. Cardiganshire Box C.
[4] NLW MS Glanpaith 285.
[5] Girth 205cm and almost unchanged in 10 years.
[6] Lewis, W.J., *Born on a Perilous Rock*. Aberystwyth (1980).

27

Pigeonsford, Rhydcolomennod

LLANGRANNOG

Precisely a mile inland and due east of the tiny seaport of Llangrannog the steep gorge carved by Nant Hawen widens sufficiently to accommodate a fine Georgian house and its pleasure grounds amidst the most picturesque of natural settings. At some 250ft above sea level, the site is sheltered well below the windswept plateau where trees are bent low by prevailing south-westerlies.

A house called Rhydcolomennod was here when the Stuarts came to the throne. The owners were of local extraction: the Parry family was followed by the Prices, who displayed upward mobility when George Price (*c.*1720–86), High Sheriff in 1759 and JP in 1767, inherited in 1752. Within three years George Price was rebuilding the façade of his house and by 1762 he was anglicizing its name to Pigeonsford. He probably made some improvement in the gardens, but an inventory of 1753 mentions agricultural elements like folds and haggards rather than pleasure grounds. His marriage to Dorothea Bowen of Llwyngwair, Pembs., in 1762 brought a useful dowry, but also some difficulties. The Bowens had Methodist sympathies and Madam Price (Dorothy as she is commemorated on a plaque on Llangrannog church) was converted, scandalizing people in the neighbourhood as she rode to chapel wearing a scarlet cloak.

George Price was succeeded in 1786 by his son, also George Price (1768–1829), JP in 1790, burgess of Cardigan in 1792, Deputy Lieutenant in 1797 and mayor of Cardigan in 1808 and 1812. International affairs impinged on this quiet corner of the county when the French unsuccessfully invaded Pembrokeshire. In 1797, as captain of the 46th Foot, George Price was called upon to escort French prisoners from Fishguard to Whitehaven. Later Col. Price of Pigeonsford was one of the local gentlemen who rushed to the aid of customs officers when a wine-laden French brig foundered on nearby Penbryn Beach in 1816. They were too late to prevent the local inhabitants from pillaging the cargo 'to such an extent that seven of them died of alcoholic poisoning and a number were excommunicated from membership of the local chapel.'[1]

George Price II married Elizabeth Bowen Jordan of Neeston, Pembs., co-heiress with her

Around 1900 Pigeonsford boasted Cardiganshire's 'tallest rhododendron'. This picture may have been taken by the keen amateur photographer Mrs. C.W.W. Hope (née Florence Lewes of Llanllŷr).

Private collection.

sisters (although her father Barrett Bowen Jordan fled to Flanders in 1784 because of debt[2]). A rare horticultural record notes that to celebrate the birth to George and Elizabeth of an heir, George Bowen Jordan Price (1806–81), a walnut tree was planted outside the drawing-room window.[3] It survived until at least the 1930s.

In a career following Cambridge and including the Royal Pembroke Artillery Militia, this third and last George Price acquired the customary suffixes of HS, JP and DL; more unusually, he changed his surname on inheriting the property of his aunt Hester, becoming Capt. George Bowen Jordan Jordan. He was particularly fond of racing, trained his horses on the clifftop above Cefn Cwrt and built new stables at Pigeonsford in 1831. This was two years after he succeeded to the estate and a year before his first marriage, to Ellen Owen of Orielton. The *Register* dates the probable remodelling of the house to 'about 1820', but the heir's circumstances make a date around 1830 seem more likely. The informative Llangrannog tithe map of 1840 shows a layout traceable today.

Ellen died in 1856, having given birth to six children and 'superintended the planting' of a red rhododendron which by the 1930s was 'one of the largest rhododendrons in the kingdom'. George next married Eleanor Powell, sister of William Beauclerk Powell, who later inherited Nanteos; there was no issue. George's heir was his grandson, a minor, Richard Price Jordan. For some years the estate was let out, and in 1908, when Capt. Richard

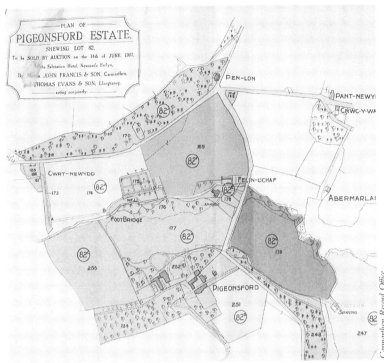

Lot 82 represented the core of the estate at the sale on 14 June 1907.

Camarthen Record Office.

Price Jordan offered it for sale, the remaining 62 acres of the ancient demesne were broken up. In the meantime the gardens had acquired a tennis lawn (considered by the auctioneer's copywriter to 'prevent stiffness in front of the homely looking Mansion') and a '"Rose Garden", tastefully set out with nice walks, one leading to the garden [i.e. the walled kitchen garden], through the shrubbery, along the end of the meadows over the rustic bridge.'

Pigeonsford house itself remained in the family: it was bought by the son of Richard's aunt, Ellen Jordan, who had married Admiral Charles Webley Hope. The new occupiers were Charles William Webley Hope and his wife Florence ('Polly') Lewes of Llanllŷr. The next sale, in 1926, was to someone of a different ilk: David Owen Evans, locally born nonconformist barrister, industrialist and Liberal MP for Cardiganshire 1932–45. His friend David Lloyd George was a frequent visitor to Pigeonsford. Another visitor, Ifan ab

Owen Edwards (later of Bryneithin), founded the celebrated camp for the Welsh youth movement Urdd Gobaith Cymru on the neighbouring farm of Cefn Cwrt, where Capt. Jordan once exercised his horses. In the 1930s D.O. Evans added on to the house a new south-west wing whose sober exterior conceals a magnificent art deco interior executed by Italian craftsmen. He also made some alterations to the adjacent garden, such as building a low terrace wall with a fountain.

Later in the 20th century the estate was further fragmented: stable block, kitchen garden and mansion came into separate ownership, and each acquired its own distinctive garden identity. The former stable courtyard, now known as Pigeonsford Farm or Rhydcolomennod, boasts well-tended box hedges of a dimension not achieved in less than a generation or two. As on the tithe map, the main access to both stables and mansion is from the adjacent unnumbered road to the east. The secondary drive extending eastwards has today dwindled to a muddy footpath beneath a hanging wood full of hart's-tongue fern and seedling trees: the remnants of a line of good beeches and fragments of stone steps attest to its former designed status.

For some years 'Pigeonsford Walled Garden', accessed via the field numbered 177 on the plan illustrated on page 77, opened in the growing season as a nursery, for plant fairs and open days. The *Register* lists the walled garden as grade II and describes it as 'a very good and well-preserved example of a large, 18th-century former kitchen garden, with impressive walls and original internal layout.' This productive garden will have served the tables of the first George Price and was kept up to standard by improvements such as concrete bed edgings in the early 20th century until it was abandoned in the 1960s. Two buildings within the garden – an old seven-sided former apple store at the south-east corner and a five-

sided brick gazebo built against the north wall in the 1930s by D.O. Evans (and visited by Lloyd George) – are considered of particular interest. Although the ground was restored to cultivation in the 1980s, and old apple trees remained, the built structures have suffered inevitable ravages of time. Ivy attacked the surrounding stone walls and the 19th-century greenhouse made by Halliday & Co., Middleton, Manchester, lost its superstructure. Happily, rescue is now in prospect. After some half-century in separate ownership, this old kitchen garden is now linked again to its 'parent house' and the fabric of its walls is to undergo restoration.

Recently the mansion has been renamed Plas Llangrannog. The pleasure grounds had become very overgrown and Pigeonsford's 'green sward' has had to be recovered by clearing thickets of rhododendron and bramble and removing diseased and damaged trees. A handful of trees and shrubs, including an evergreen oak *Quercus ilex* and miscellaneous rhododendrons and azaleas, remain from those described in the 1908 sale particulars: a grafted manna ash *Fraxinus ornus*, now stunted, is one of the more interesting species. As at Nanteos and Llanerchaeron, pets' graves are a reminder of past occupants' sentiment. More than usually elaborate gravestones commemorate two dogs, and an even grander one marks 'Poor Dolly', the favourite mare of G.B.J. Jordan. The mansion is currently undergoing thorough restoration, and if eventual refurbishment of its garden setting reflects a fraction of the care expended on the building, the result will be remarkable.

The entire estate is in private ownership and not open to visitors.   *P.D.*

[1] Jenkins, J. Geraint, 'Penbryn Beach', in *Ceredigion* IX, 4 (1983) p. 348.
[2] Jones, Francis, *Historic Houses of Pembrokeshire* (1996).
[3] Hope, Evelyn, *Llangranog and the Pigeonsford Family* Cardigan (1931).

Tanybwlch

LLANYCHAEARN

The mansion at Tanybwlch is barely visible today, nestling in a dense native woodland on the northern flank of Alltwen, the cliff which terminates the arc of shingle beach where the Ystwyth river reaches the sea. In 1825 there was a farm there, which was bought by Maj.-Gen. Lewis Davies, eighth child and fourth son of John Davies of Crugiau, a small mansion on opposite side of the Ystwyth valley. Maj.- Gen. Davies had done well in life: he had married an heiress, Jane Davies of Cwmcynfelin, and had had a successful military career, in the West Indies in the 1790s, and in Europe during the Napoleonic wars. His four children were all born at Cwmcynfelin, and although he owned some land in Llanbadarn Fawr and Llanychaearn parishes he seems for most of his life to have remained domiciled at his wife's home. His house must have been only recently completed in 1828 when he died there. His widow remained there until her son Matthew married in 1832.

The house Lewis Davies erected at Tanybwlch was a handsome, lime-rendered, six-bedroomed, square building centred upon an elegant stone staircase, top-lit by an octagonal roof light. There were two spurs, servants' offices and stabling to the rear, and a lozenge-shaped walled garden on flat ground at the extreme eastern margin of his 130 acres. The sloping plantations behind the house were cut by two swathes to create 'lights', narrow clearings by which sunlight could penetrate to the buildings at the foot of the north-facing slope. The 300 metres to the door into the walled garden could be approached by contoured footpaths through the small pleasure ground south-east of the house, and along these paths rough-hewn embayments accommodated seats with an outlook to the sea. Paths also

28

Plas Tanybwlch and the rather exaggerated cliff of Alltwen. Watercolour, 1869. NLW Drawing Vol. 29.

followed the contour along from the house through a plantation on the flank of Alltwen cliff. Although overgrown by the more robust shrubbery plants like cherry laurel and rhododendrons, the bones of the pleasure ground, and the buttressed stone garden walls remain. There were no early greenhouses, nor a brick-lined fruit wall, but in this sheltered spot so close to sea level, the garden, which survives today, is quite warm. A small gardeners' cottage was, in the mid 19th century, built on to the external south-west corner of the garden wall.

A second phase of improvement came when the major-general's grandson, Matthew Lewis Vaughan Davies, reached the age of 21 and claimed his inheritance in 1861. One of his first moves was to buy the adjoining Tanycastell farm from W.T.R. Powell of Nanteos, thus more than doubling the parcel of land around the mansion and opening the way to demolish the old Tanybwlch farm buildings near the mansion, and to redesign his approach drive such that it no longer passed through Tanycastell farmyard. Partly through inheritance from childless cousins and uncles, the fortunes of the family had increased, and Vaughan Davies owned a total of 3674 acres, yielding £974 annually.[1] Because much of this acreage consisted of sheepwalks of no great value, his income from land ranked him as 23rd in the county. Soon he was a JP, active in local affairs, rebuilding the Tanybwlch bridge at Rhydyfelin, razing and rebuilding Llanychaearn church, and standing for the Conservative seat in 1880 and 1885.

It was as a result of his marriage, at the age of 48 to the wealthy 50-year-old widow Mary Maples Jenkins, that the estate underwent a third major phase of change. Not only was the house doubled in size, clad in rock-dressed stone and embellished with castellations above the entrance, but a large stable block was built in the orchard adjoining the walled garden. A convenient arch through the garden wall adjoining the front door of the now-enlarged gardener's cottage at the corner allowed horse-manure to be transported efficiently from stables to the manure space adjoining the kitchen garden. The main drive was remodelled to bypass Tanycastell farm and contour the east flank of Castell hill, and a new laundry and gamekeeper's cottage was erected opposite Llanychaearn church to take advantage of the abundant spring-water supply near by. A new footpath hugging the river bank was built along the south margin of the Ystwyth from Tanycastell to the sea, and at the foot of Alltwen a Tea Cottage, also rock-dressed and castellated, was erected where visitors could take tea after a pleasant stroll from the house. Today the site is indicated by the cut-off railings surrounding the cottage, and the traces of a rockery rich in primroses in the cliff behind.

The Tea Cottage, a two-storey house, cost £215 to build in 1891. Photo album 711.

Those were great days for the walled garden. New greenhouses were ordered and erected, the three doors to the garden fitted with locks, and plants were ordered from the famous nurseries of James Backhouse & Son of York. Mrs Vaughan Davies sent her gardener packages of campanulas, asters, penstemons and sweet peas. In 1909 the gardener, Younds, protested that 'there is no more room in the garden for any more seeds of flowering plants.' None the less, fifteen new young trees including four climbers were sent to the bailiff. Climbers adorned the walls on either side of the front door. Also in the garden were cold frames devoted to violets donated by Mrs Powell of Nanteos.

From 1895 until 1921 Matthew Lewis Vaughan Davies held the Liberal seat for Cardiganshire and he and his wife were extremely active in local political and university life. Their twenty bedrooms must have allowed them to entertain in considerable style, and the gardens played their part in supplying entertainment, nourishment and flowers. The old Tanybwlch farm buildings below the drive were demolished, and the site was levelled for a grass tennis court, for which a new mower was ordered in 1909.

It was not until he was 81, in 1921, that Matthew Lewis Vaughan Davies was elevated to the peerage, taking the title of Lord Ystwyth. By now his wife was too old and ill to take much part in public affairs. They may never quite have managed to lure royalty into their home, but at least in 1933 Prince Albert, the future king, landed his plane on the Tanybwlch flats *en route* to the Royal Welsh Show at Aberystwyth, and posed for photographs with the aged peer on his own front doorstep. *C.P.*

[1] Owners of Land. Wales 1871. Published 1875.

Also see:
Palmer, C., 'A History of the Tanybwlch Estate' in *Ceredigion* XIV, 1 (2001) pp. 37–78.

Trawsgoed, Crosswood
LLANAFAN

29

One of the four great estates of Cardiganshire, Trawsgoed is situated in the lower Ystwyth valley, six miles from the coast, where the river occupies a broad fertile valley. Not far upstream, the valley becomes steep-sided, a gorge in places, foreshadowing the terrain of Johnes's Hafod landscape to the east.

Trawsgoed has belonged to the Vaughan family since the 13th century, though until the 16th century it was little more than a farm. At the death, in 1635, of Edward Vaughan (High Sheriff of Cardiganshire 1619), it had grown to be the largest estate in the county. His son acquired a knighthood but lost much of the fabric of his house to the Roundheads and was obliged to rebuild. Sir John's grandson became 1st Viscount Lisburne, and, two generations later, the 4th viscount was elevated to an earldom in 1776. The estate passed down to the 7th earl, who sold it to the Ministry of Agriculture, Fisheries and Food in 1947.

Thomas Dineley's sketch c. 1684.

There is little to be seen today which reflects the early design of Trawsgoed, but some useful documents survive. The Duke of Beaufort included Trawsgoed on his itinerary through Wales in 1684, and as a result we have Thomas Dineley's sketch of what was probably the south-west face of Sir John Vaughan's Trawsgoed.[1] An estate survey of 1756 gives an image of the north-east face of the house, which looked out on to two symmetrical plats of lawn within a walled and gated enclosure. In line with this central axis, an avenue reached out north-eastward of the house and penetrated a 144-acre palisaded deer park on the rising ground beyond. To the north-west of the mansion was an asymmetric kitchen garden, while to the south-east and south-west were formal gardens quartered into beds or lawns by geometric paths. Avenues, probably of oaks, also projected radially to the south-east and the north-west.

By 1771 Henry Mercier's map of the demesne shows the house set in a densely designed rectangular area with kitchen garden to the north-west, an ornamental court to the north-east and a formal garden with radial beds centred upon a circular pond to the south-west.[2] The south-east sector contained a shrubbery or wilderness threaded with sinuous paths, and a bowling green. Wilmot Vaughan, 4th viscount and 1st earl, had inherited in 1764, but was already resident principally at Mamhead in Devon, which his infant son by his deceased wife, Elizabeth Nightingale, had recently inherited. Vaughan commissioned Robert Adam to alter Mamhead mansion and 'Capability' Brown to redesign its garden. At Trawsgoed in 1771 he obtained suggestions for estate improvement from J. Probert, Steward to Earl Powis. (Probert also improved the castle grounds at Aberystwyth, which he leased from Thomas Johnes of Hafod.[3]) The work was overseen by the agent, Edward Hughes of Aberllolwyn. In 1788 Vaughan was giving instructions that hedges be removed on either side of the avenue of oaks, to create the appearance of one great lawn. Like other landowners he was an investor in the turnpike trust and will have had influence upon the routing of the present B4340 along the east bank of the Ystwyth from Abermagwr to

Detail of the 'Map of a part of Crosswood Demesne' by Henry Mercier, 1771. (Also see front cover of this book.)

Llanafan in the 1790s, thus removing the public road from across his park.

Wilmot Vaughan died in 1800, having rarely visited Trawsgoed. Malkin, writing in 1802, remarked:

> For many years this venerable mansion has been altogether neglected and has consequently fallen into decay. The late Lord Lisburne was so much attached to his beautiful seat in Devonshire that he never visited Crosswood Park, but for a short time, when county politics required his attendance… The house, as in the former instance [Nanteos], is set down in an obscure corner of the park, and though large, is laid out in a number of confined and inconvenient apartments.

Malkin recorded that the earl's second son Col. John Vaughan was 'a very recent inhabitant' and having taken 1600 acres in hand, that he looked forward to 'rendering this neglected estate a paradise'. (His elder brother, the insane Wilmot III, retained the title, and Mamhead.)

For Col. John Vaughan, with his wife and young family, Trawsgoed offered great possibilities, facilitated, as elsewhere in the county, by the creation of new turnpike roads. Most of the changes observable on the tithe

map took place during his life or that of his son, the 4th earl. By 1845 the old deer park pale was swept away, as was the avenue across the park and a farm and hedgerows to the east, to create an extensive landscape park with a few mature scattered oaks. A new approach to the mansion left the turnpike road opposite Birchgrove and curved eastward through a grove of what have become venerable English oaks and sweet chestnuts, to approach the front of the house, where a turning circle was laid out, bounded from the park by a ha-ha. The southern, serpentine drive led off eastward from this point. Close by, a tree nursery supplied the seedlings for improving the estate. Along the margin of the new turnpike, screening plantations were established, and within the gardens, the formal compartments (with the exception of the pond) were swept away, and the kitchen gardens enlarged to their present shape. On inheriting the earldom in 1820, Col. Vaughan sold Mamhead, and with the proceeds was able to get out of debt and return from exile in France. Either he, or his son, the 4th earl, built the splendid and ornate library which protrudes from the south-west façade. Samuel Lewis visited Trawsgoed in 1843; his account indicates considerable changes since Malkin's visit, describing it as a modern mansion.

Substantial estate improvements were carried out by the 5th earl (1873–88), with loans from the Land Improvement Company. The Victorian garden is, however, chiefly the legacy of the 6th earl (1888–99), in whose time it is recorded that the gardens were relaid and terraced and ornamented with fountains and summerhouses and hothouses. He also added the large château-style service wing, by Thomas Aldwinkle, in 1891. The 25-inch OS map of 1887, an article of 1891 in *The Journal of Horticulture and Cottage Gardener*[4], and family photograph albums, give a full record. The walled kitchen garden now contained a lean-to greenhouse on the north-west wall and three additional glasshouses, the largest of which is described in an inventory as containing rhododendrons, azaleas, carnations, gardenias, many plants in pots and the earl's collection of 415 orchids. The paths were flanked with pyramid apples and pears, and the walls with cherry, peach and a fig tree which still survives today. A semi-circular enclosure north-west of the kitchen-garden was devoted to beekeeping. The formal garden south-west of the house was remodelled as lawn with a deep central fishpool and fountain surrounded by vases containing palms and formal bedding borders margined with rope-edged artificial stone tiles by Pulham of Broxbourne. To the north-west side of the lawn was a conservatory displaying flowers in season brought in from the glasshouses in the kitchen gardens beyond. The article also mentions a rose walk leading to the summerhouse, and to the extensive tennis lawns. The lime avenue along the main drive was quite young at this time.

The other major Victorian embellishment was the creation of an arboretum in the two former fields to the south-west; formerly the garden ended at a transverse row of limes crossing the end of the lawn. The new planting, described as 'planned' in the article of 1891, created an axis of monkey puzzles *Araucaria araucana* leading to the huge hiba *Thujopsis dolabrata* which rises above a curved stone bench with griffon supports. New ornamental steps descending to the arboretum were adorned with statuary, stone dragons and heraldic beasts. The arboretum was planted with an extensive collection of newly fashionable exotic species and their cultivars, with particular emphasis on the genera *Chamaecyparis* and *Thuja*, their species and varieties including *Chamaecyparis lawsoniana*, *C. nootkatensis*, *C. pisifera* 'Squarrosa', *C. obtusa*, *Thuja plicata*, *T. occidentalis* and hybrids. Other important conifers include *Cedrus atlantica*

Trawsgoed: the summerhouse beneath the oak, c. 1891. Photo Album 819.

New concrete paving on the garden front,
photographed for Country Life in 1938.

glauca, *Cryptomeria japonica, Cupressus glabra, Calocedrus decurrens, Pinus wallichiana, Pseudotsuga menziesii, Sequoiadendron giganteum* and *Tsuga heterophylla*, in addition to some very fine broadleaf trees such as the cut-leaved beech *Fagus sylvatica asplenifolia*, the weeping beech *F.s. pendula* and the copper beech *F.s. purpurea*. Wellingtonias were also planted at marginal positions near drives.[5] There is also a diverse shrubbery containing some interesting rhododendrons including hybrids 'Loder's White', 'Pink Pearl', 'Discolor' and 'Cynthia' and species *nobleanum, augustinii, cheiranthifolium* and *auriculatum*. Large azaleas, hollies, kalmias, skimmias and heathers were dug up and transplanted as the work progressed.

In the interwar years the 7th earl remodelled the garden to the north-east front, with boundary wall and gates, echoing the Dineley sketch, on the top of the ha-ha. He also introduced the tradition of ceremonial tree planting. Two *Quercus robur* south-east of the mansion were planted by himself, and by Alice Countess Amherst his grandmother, (the widow of the 5th Earl) on 8 February 1913 and are marked by plaques. Subsequent plantings commemorate visits by HRH the Prince of Wales (30 October 1923) and the Right Hon. Stanley Baldwin (25 October 1928). The 7th earl's wife, Regina, Countess of Lisburne created the Japanese water garden which is fed by a channel leading from a concrete tank in the woodland south-east of the mansion to a pool on the edge of the main lawn. It included a Japanese bridge, a rockwork cascade and a pool ornamented with pelican, stork, crocodile and Japanese lantern. She also made the trellised rose garden at the foot of the geometric terraces laid out by the 6th earl. In 1938 the gravelled paths south-west of the mansion were replaced with concrete paving, cast *in situ* to create the appearance of large individual slabs. This was a new technique at the time and led to a commercial feature in the magazine *Country Life*[6].

Since the Welsh Office Agriculture Department left Trawsgoed in 1995 it has been acquired by a development company in which the 8th earl's younger son, John, has an interest, and the service wing has been divided into flats. Much of the landscape setting is managed as farmland, the walled garden has been divided, and the south-west garden and arboretum are suffering from neglect.   *C.P.*

[1] Dineley (1684).
[2] NLW MSS CD 111, 23B.
[3] Nicholson, G., *The Cambrian Traveller's Guide*, 2nd Ed., London (1813).
[4] 'Crosswood Park' in *Journal of Horticulture and Cottage Gardener* 12 March 1891 p. 209-210.
[5] The Welsh Historic Gardens Trust carried out a detailed tree survey measuring 317 trees in 1994.
[6] 'Concrete in the Garden', in *Country Life*, 12.3.1938, p. cxii.

Also see:
Morgan, G., *A Welsh House and its Family, the Vaughans of Trawsgoed*, Llandysul (1997).

30

Tŷglyn
LLANDDEWI ABER-ARTH

This small estate is less than two miles upstream of Llanerchaeron at the point where the Nant Camel joins the Aeron. In addition to farming, the advantages of the situation were a water mill powered by a leat off the Aeron, and fish traps for catching sewin on their migration upriver to breed. A house was built on the site by Llewellyn Thomas Parry in the early 17th century, and a wall-mounted sundial bearing the year 1624 survives in a new position in the gable end of the barn nearest the house. It was presumably moved there during the major remodelling of the house which was carried out after Henry Jones inherited the estate in 1750.

There is an excellent estate plan of 1759 which was drawn for owner Henry Jones.[1] The house looked out westward on to a formal space, beyond which were three enclosures. To one side was the farmyard, with a rickyard, and to the other a rectangular enclosed garden. Orchards occupied the flat land adjoining the Aeron and its tributary the Camel, and the woods extending westward were known as The Walks, which implies their use as a pleasure ground. It is likely that Henry Jones planted the lime avenue which extends westward from the house and ended in a rustic bower. His daughter Susannah was there in 1796, mulling over the marriage proposal of her cousin the Revd Alban Thomas. 'I ... enjoy a solitary walk to the bower, and recollect our conversation, and have twice gone so far as to wish you were there with me.' They were married in 1797 and her husband added her

Engraving reproduced from Nicholas (1872).

surname to his own. With the later inheritance of the nearby Monachty estate in 1804 he added another, thus becoming the Revd Alban Thomas Jones Gwynne, the man whose very substantial fortune was to result in the building of the harbour at Aberaeron. The Gwynne fortune in gold bullion was transferred with difficulty, by horse-drawn sled, from Monachty to Tŷglyn, and in 1808 a chapel was appended to the south end of the house.

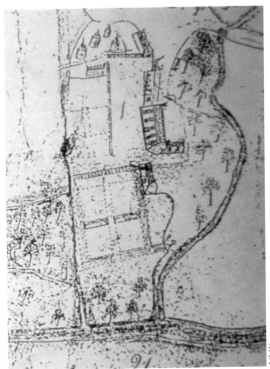

'An Accurate Survey of Tuglyn Demesne the Estate of Henry Jones Esq., by Stephen Saunders', 1759.

Tŷglyn: the garden house at the corner of the newly restored garden.

CDP 2000

The second major influence on the garden was that of the Revd Alban Thomas's grandson, Alban Thomas Davies, a captain in the East India Company, who inherited in 1830. The details of a great variety of new plantings of ornamental trees and named fruit tree cultivars are itemized in a manuscript notebook which spanned the years from 1835 to 1859.[2] Plants were obtained from Bristol nurseries Garraways and Sons, W. Monk, and H. Maule and Son. Notes within the gardener's books reveal many details of this garden's productivity with its beds for asparagus, coltsfoot and sea kale, and its yields of potatoes, cabbage, radish, rhubarb and other garden vegetables.

During the Captain's tenure, the garden wall was extended westward around the existing orchard, and along the bank of the Aeron, probably adding to the frost problems of the site. A small two-storey garden house was added at the south-east corner. The farm buildings were also altered and extended, and an unusual granary raised on staddle-stones was added to the farmyard. A door, now blocked, in the north wall of the western garden was known as the hop garden door. This hop garden would have supplied the raw material for the brewhouse which adjoins the house. When the estate was sold in 1883, the catalogue described 'Gardens, Orchards, Pleasure grounds and Woodland walks adjoining the River Aeron, with beautifully laid out grounds, shrubberies, and extensive gardens well stocked with the choicest fruit trees … Ornamental walks from the residence down to and for a considerable distance along the margins of the River Aeron …'

The productive walled garden was maintained until the 1950s, when it fell into neglect. It has been restored by the Tŷ Glyn Davis Trust with the support of the National Lottery Community Fund as a garden 'for the use of families of children with disabilities. While this is not a historic re-creation, it has been possible to use the 19th-century gardener's book to replant many of the original cultivars within this garden.[3]

The trees in the surrounding grounds reflect the 200-year history of this site. Oldest are a massive sycamore (girth 521cm) between the house and the road bridge, certain beeches, and some of the limes on the walk west of the house. More exotic plantings of conifers east of the Camel probably reflect Capt. Alban Thomas Davies's tenure and include wellingtonias, Douglas firs, *Thuja plicata*, *Thujopsis dolabrata*, *Abies nordmanniana*, *Cedrus atlantica*, and the coast redwood, *Sequoia sempervirens*. Until recently there was also an umbrella pine *Sciadopitys verticillata*.[4] A more recently planted and unusual tree is distinctively fragrant balsam poplar *Populus balsamifera* south of the house.   C.P.

[1] NLW Map PB 4340.
[2] NLW MS Minor Lists 19, Tŷglyn 45.
[3] R.L. Laidlaw, pers. comm.
[4] A.O. Chater, notes on visit March/April 1992.

Ynyshir

LLANFIHANGEL GENAU'R-GLYN, YSGUBOR Y COED

Ynyshir lies in the lea of one of the lozenges of wooded rocky outcrop which follow the strike of the land and characterize the topography south of the Dyfi estuary. A similar outcrop is crowned by the house at Lodge Park, its position betraying its earlier origins as a hunting lodge. At Ynyshir, by contrast, the house was always residential, and its situation to the east of the outcrop provides shelter from the ravages of westerly gales.

This has been a house of substance since the early 17th century when Ynyshir was the home of David Lloyd, and then his son John, who is commemorated over the south window of Eglwysfach church for its erection in 1623. John's son Thomas married Alice Pryse, and through their daughter Dorothy, the estate passed to her husband John Knowles, High Sheriff of Cardiganshire in 1698. Few traces of the 17th-century landscaping remain today, but, as at Lodge Park, there seems to have been some formal planting of oaks. An avenue of trees ran northward along the strike of the outcrop west of the mansion, and another double row ran east–west across the low land east of Cae'r berllan.[1] These axes do not seem to have aligned with views from the house site but may have marked significant rides in the landscape.

In the 18th century Ynyshir passed through a female line of inheritance to Mrs Skryme of Pembrokeshire, who sold large tracts of land in the area to neighbouring landowner Edward Jeffreys of Dovey Castle and Ynyshir itself to the tenant, John Hughes. Meyrick described it in 1809 as 'a large old-fashioned house'. Hughes in 1780 sold it to Matthew Davies of Cwmcynfelin, and thus it became a part of the inheritance of the Cwmcynfelin heiress Jane

A detail of the tithe map (1845).

Davies, wife of Maj.-Gen. Lewis Davies of Tanybwlch. On her death in 1840 she left all her land in Ysgubor y Coed to her second son the Revd Lewis Charles Davies, who promptly married the next year. The tithe survey of 1845 shows that the Revd Mr Davies now occupied Ynyshir with 524 acres in hand and also owned a further 890 acres in four tenanted farms and the plantations and mill at Furnace. Jointly with his neighbour George Jeffreys he invested in the reclamation of salt marsh 'marian' on the margin of the Dyfi and in furnishing mortgages to less prosperous local gentry[2]. It seems likely that he was living at Ynyshir in 1851, although on census night only his eight-year-old daughter, her governess and five house servants were at home. From 1864 until his death in 1876 he was resident near Wincanton, as rector of Charleton Musgrove, but he remained a substantial landowner in Cardiganshire, with 3153 acres yielding an annual rental of £898.[3]

31

In 1871 Ynyshir was leased to George Cosens, his wife and infant children. Cosens was later to live at Cwmcynfelin, and then to build the new villa, Bronpadarn, near Aberystwyth.

Lewis Charles Davies's death in 1876 probably precipitated the sale of Ynyshir. By the time of the censuses of 1881 and 1891 Ynyshir was owned by George Paddock, a local solicitor and magistrate, and in 1903 it was purchased by Major James Barry Taunton, a High Sheriff of Cardiganshire.

In 1910 it was bought by Thomas Oliver Cross, of Alderley Edge, Cheshire, a surveyor and civil engineer whose family fortune derived from mines and docks. T.O. Cross died in 1929 and the estate was purchased by William Hubert Mappin, of the jewellery family of Mappin and Webb, who died in 1966. Anxious to protect the estate in perpetuity from inappropriate development, Mappin set up a Deed of Covenant whereby the National Trust would exert influence upon future use. After his death, and in line with his conservation wishes, much of the land was sold to the RSPB, and the Ynyshir Reserve opened in 1970. The house and 14 acres of garden has become a renowned hotel in the ownership of Mr and Mrs Reen, who take great pride in the garden.

The tithe survey map of 1845 shows the house and grounds much as the Revd Lewis Davies inherited them. The old house had three ancillary buildings to the east of it and the group was enclosed by woodland to west and north and by a ha-ha to the east. The farm buildings were approached through the yard adjoining the main house. At this time there is no indication of a walled kitchen garden, and the evidence of successive censuses indicates that the enclosures beside the dwellings of Ynys Edwin were concerned with sheep management, not gardening. Two footpaths ran northward through the woodland and a small stream descending the slope drained eastward past a small elongated, wooded outcrop. Bounded by this stream, and by the ha-ha, was a low-lying field named Cae Bach. There is one pollarded oak at the north extremity of the present garden which is 518cm girth, and likely to be in excess of 200 years in age. There is also a very large lime *Tilia cordata* (girth 369cm) a little to the north-west.

It seems probable that the Revd Lewis Charles Davies made improvements to the grounds in the fashion of the 1850s and 1860s. The woodland north of the house became a pleasure ground, laced with a network of footpaths margined with boulders of white quartzite. This area today contains oak, beech and sweet chestnut with a shrubby evergreen understorey of lanky outgrown English yew, box, cherry laurel, *Rhododendron ponticum* and butcher's broom. The stream descending the slope was formed into a narrow, stepped, quartzite-margined cascade.

A more ostentatious phase of improvement arose from George Paddock's occupancy in the 1880s. Paddock's Staffordshire-born wife Annie may also have been a substantial horticultural influence. By the time of the OS 25-inch survey (1888) nineteen specimen trees had been planted in Cae Bach. These include *Abies nordmanniana*, *A. pinsapo*, *Cedrus atlantica glauca*, *Pinus nigra* and *P. sylvestris*, fine specimens of Douglas firs, wellingtonias and an *Acer platanoides*. The old pleasure ground was laced with footpaths and there was a stepway rising west of the house which led the visitor west and then south to a timber summerhouse in a triangular walled enclosure set in a clearing at a high point on the ridge. There was a pheasantry in the wood north of the house, and Douglas firs were also planted in the margins of the pleasure ground. The scattered buildings east of the house had been cleared away and replaced by fountains in the lawn within the ha-ha. South of the service courtyard a triangular walled kitchen garden was built in

Ynyshir garden during the ownership of T.O. Cross (1910–29). The glasshouses date from George Paddock's time.

the space cut off by a new access drive to the farm. The old curving avenue of Scots pines was superseded by a more direct approach from the east. At the confluence of the two drives is a one-storey stone lodge with red-brick window-dressings and reddish sandstone quoins. Within the gates, the new drive approaching the house was margined by a mixed planting of conifers and deciduous trees.

The old house itself was also enlarged, and embellished at its southern end by a linked group of three ornamental glasshouses, two rectangular and one circular, which together looked out on to a lawned platform and fountain. This conservatory and its communicating vinery must have been George's or perhaps his wife Annie's pride and joy. In the sale catalogue of 1903 it is described as being fitted with a new boiler, and an acetylene gas plant for lighting. Beside the drive to the house were large-flowered hybrid rhododendrons and tightly clipped shrubs, and a margin of quartzite boulders.

George Paddock died in 1895 aged 73 and was survived by his wife. The estate and its two stock farms Ynyshir and Ynys Edwin were auctioned in 1903 as seven lots. The 162 acres sold with the house are described as 'valuable and highly ornamental woods and plantation of oak, larch, scots fir, spruce, ash and other species, affording shady walks and secluded retreats, and at the same time forming grand cover for game'. Along with the fishing on the Einion and the Dyfi, the unrivalled wildfowl shooting on the marshes and the proximity of the Gogerddan and the Machynlleth hounds, this was described as the ideal domain for a sporting gentleman.

Thomas Oliver Cross was just such a gentleman, and kept the most meticulous game-books from 1911 to 1924. His papers indicate a regular friendship with hunting squire Lewes T. Loveden Pryse of Gogerddan. He lived at Ynyshir with his wife and daughter Edie, and kept a family album. During this period the previously stark rendered house

Ynyshir: the large pollarded oak at the north end of the garden.

CDP 2004

became enrobed in Virginia creeper and the gardens were lush with broad herbaceous borders and luxuriant island beds of gladioli and dahlias in the sloping lawns.[4]

In 1903 Cae Bach with its parkland trees had been described as 'the front meadow'. Part of it was fenced off as an additional kitchen garden and part was a tennis lawn. Animals were excluded by railings and the substantial drainage ditch on the east margin. It was not until the 1930s, when the bachelor W.H. Mappin bought the estate, that Cae Bach, the small wooded outcrop, and the field to the north of it, Dol y Bont Issa, were formed into an informal 6.5-acre plantsman's garden below the old pleasure ground. He employed the landscape architect Lawrence of Shrewsbury who created a serene sweep of lawn in which flowing island beds led the eye to the Merioneth hills beyond.

The stream traversing the meadow was led northward to a pond with marginal planting of skunk cabbage *Lysichiton americanus* and patches of bamboo *Sasa palmata*. Most of the ha-ha was demolished to allow a gentle slope to the spreading lawns to the east. The island beds were planted with well-chosen trees, shrubs and herbaceous plants. Particularly notable is a very fine spreading *Parrotia persica*, a snow gum *Eucalyptus niphophila,* and several large clumps of the unusual shrub *Leucothoë fontanesiana* near by and in the woods. Individual island beds displayed separate drifts of hemerocallis and pampas grass, hydrangeas, and mixed shrubs. A heather garden was created on the rocky outcrop which hitherto had been clothed in mature deciduous trees. A single old beech survives on its southern flank. On the north- and south-facing slopes are pleasing groves of *Chamaecyparis pisifera* 'Squarrosa', and on the west flank some fine mature rhododendrons. The top of this outcrop made an excellent vantage point and was clothed until recently in a wilderness of *Gaultheria shallon*. This had become very overgrown and was recently removed. The outlook from here has also changed, for the RSPB has recently created a large irregular wildlife pool north of the garden.

The Paddocks' range of formal glasshouses are now gone, and the walled garden has lost the greenhouses and violet-frame recollected by Mrs Condry.[5] The large horse chestnut in front of the mansion came down in the 1960s whilst other losses and later planting have somewhat obscured the clean lines of Mappin's island beds. A recent initiative in the garden is the path and the timber Japanese bridge at the foot of the 19th-century cascade.   *C.P.*

[1] OS 25-inch Merioneth XLIX. 5 1st Ed 1888.
[2] NLW MS Cymerau deposit 24–27.
[3] Owners of Land, Wales, 1871. Published 1875.
[4] Papers in possession of Mr and Mrs Reen, Ynyshir Hall.
[5] Penny Condry, pers. comm.

Gazetteer & Index of Ceredigion Gardens

The list of parks and gardens is based on properties mentioned in historic maps and in the literature: principal books are indicated in the Bibliography on page 94. Inclusion of a site represents historic evidence: some gardens will have entirely disappeared or may yield only archaeological traces.

All grid references in Ceredigion are prefixed by 'SN'. Alternative site names are indexed and cross-referenced: names in **bold face** mean that the garden is one of those selected for detailed description in the previous pages (page numbers also in **bold**). The name of the parish in which the site is located is given in SMALL CAPITALS. These parishes are those extant at the time of the tithe survey, which spanned 1839–45 in Cardiganshire. Some parishes, such as Eglwysfach, were established subsequently, and certain other boundaries and designations may have changed with the 20th-century establishment of civil parishes, or community councils as they are now known in Wales.

Apart from the fact that some sites have been renamed by different owners, or have both Welsh and English versions of the name, the spelling of Welsh placenames is notoriously variable since they were standardized only in the mid 20th century. We have generally tried to use the forms of names preferred by owners, but have noted and cross-referenced the principal alternative forms.   *R.L.*

Bibliography

Baker-Jones, Leslie, *Princelings, Privilege and Power: the Tivyside Gentry in their Community*, Llandysul, 1999.

Cadw/ICOMOS UK, *Carmarthenshire, Ceredigion and Pembrokeshire Register of Landscapes, Parks and Gardens of special historic interest in Wales*, Cardiff, 2002.

Carlisle, Nicholas, *A Topographical Dictionary of the Dominion of Wales*, London, 1811.

Davies, Elwyn (ed.), *A Gazetteer of Welsh Place-Names*, Cardiff, 1967.

Dineley, Thomas *The account of the Official Progress of the first Duke of Beaufort through Wales 1684* (ed. R.W. Banks), London, 1888.

Eyre Evans, George, *Cardiganshire; A personal survey of some of the Antiquities, Chapels, Churches, Fonts, Plate and registers*, Aberystwyth, 1903.

Fenton, Richard, *Tours in Wales 1804-1813* (ed. J. Fisher), Cambrian Archaeological Association, London, 1917.

Horsfall-Turner, E.R., *Walks and Wanderings in County Cardigan: being a descriptive sketch of its picturesque, historic, antiquarian, romantic and traditional features*, Bingley, 1902.

Jones, Francis, *Historic Cardiganshire Homes and their Families*, Newport, 2000.

Lewis, Samuel, *A Topographical Dictionary of Wales*, Vols I & II, London, 1833, 4th ed. 1849.

Malkin, Benjamin Heath, *The Scenery, Antiquities and Bibliography of South Wales*, 2nd ed., London, 1807.

Mavor, Dr William Fordyce, *A Tour through Wales in the Summer of 1805*, London, 1809.

Meyrick, Samuel Rush, *The History and Antiquities of the County of Cardiganshire*, London, 1810, 2nd ed. Brecon,1907.

Nicholas, Thomas, *Annals and Antiquities of the Counties and County Families of Wales*, Vols I & II, London, 1872.

Richards, Melville, *Welsh Administrative and Territorial Units*, Cardiff, 1969.

Roscoe, Thomas, *Wanderings and Excursions in South Wales including the course of the Wye*, London, 1837.

General Index